AIMS IN EDUCATION
THE PHILOSOPHIC APPROACH

Aims in Education

THE PHILOSOPHIC APPROACH

edited by

T. H. B. HOLLINS

for the

SCHOOL OF EDUCATION
UNIVERSITY OF MANCHESTER

MANCHESTER
UNIVERSITY PRESS

Printed in Great Britain by Butler & Tanner Ltd, Frome and London

CONTENTS

LB
41
.H68
1966

FOREWORD

THOSE concerned with and involved in the training of teachers too frequently find themselves so immersed in the day-to-day problems of organization, administration and teaching that they seem to have little opportunity to stand back from their work and attempt to view it in its totality. The content of the training course is the product of many influences, of which historical accident is by no means the least. Education, at all levels, tends to be strongly conservative. This is perhaps inevitable, since one of its primary aims has been, and must continue to be, the conservation of the best of the past. Such a tendency, however, carries within it the danger that the system may also conserve elements that are less than the best and, in particular, elements which once were relevant but which, in the modern world and radically changed social environment, serve needs which no longer exist or are aimed at goals which have become outmoded or transformed. The best defence against this insidious inertia and comfortable self-satisfaction with the *status quo* is a constant re-examination of the basic aims of education, and critical re-appraisal of content and method in the light of such re-examination. A survey of current writing—and speaking—in education does not suggest any reluctance on the part of educationists to adumbrate on the aims of education, however. Indeed, the educational platform seems to possess a built-in stimulus to pontification, so frequently does it trigger-off immensely weighty pronouncements on aims and values. And yet a closer examination of the products of this reflexology reveals little but the 'gaseous clouds of platitude and lay sermonizing' mentioned by Mr. Hollins in his introduction to this book, and practically none of the 'stringently self-critical and logically consistent thinking' asked for by Mr. Harrison. This was one of the reasons which led the School of Education to organize the series of lectures which are reproduced in this volume, and why we chose 'the philosophic approach' as the subtitle to the series. We hoped that our speakers would demonstrate the value of rigorous, critical thought as applied to the aims of the educational process, believing that the current diet of students of education contains too much pap and not enough roughage.[1]

We had a further reason for believing that our general aim was useful. One of the significant aspects of the contemporary world is its emphasis on scientific discovery and development. Our students are more conscious than ever before of the immense changes caused by, and promised by, scientific research. An increasing number of teachers in training are looking to educational research to transform the educational system. Some of them are extremists, believing that *all* our problems can be solved by the educational psychologist, not realizing the limitations of research in that part of the socio-political field called 'education'. Basic problems of aims and values must be determined before the researchers are called in to advise us how (or even if) particular aims may be achieved. The philosophy of education thus possesses a primacy and importance that cannot be yielded to educational psychology and educational sociology. And it is essential that our scientifically-minded students be brought to appreciate this—and to appreciate also that the rigour,

[1] To those who suspect this metaphor, and who are tempted to point out the undoubted food-value of pap, may we suggest that an unrestricted diet of milk-pudding produces costiveness. The value of roughage is to tune up the whole system and make it more active and efficient.

precision and exactitude of thought displayed by the true educational philosopher is every bit as demanding as that involved in scientific method.

This is the second volume of public lectures produced by the University of Manchester School of Education. The first[1] was generously received by the critics. I have no doubt that this collection will equally serve a need. We are grateful to Mr. Hollins for undertaking the editing of the lectures, a task which was the less onerous, I fancy, because of the precision of thought and writing on the part of the contributors. To them I should like to offer our apologies for the delay in publication, which is in no sense the responsibility of the lecturers themselves.

May I take this opportunity of thanking those who very kindly acted as chairmen at the lectures: Miss M. D. Higginson, Headmistress, Bolton School; Professor R. A. C. Oliver, Professor A. N. Prior and Professor B. A. Wortley, University of Manchester. We join in the universal regret at the death of one of our chairmen, the late Professor D. P. Costello.

STEPHEN WISEMAN

[1] *Examinations and English Education*, edited by S. Wiseman, Manchester University Press, 1961.

INTRODUCTION

by

T. H. B. HOLLINS

The School of Education of Manchester University invited a number of philosophers and educationists to contribute to a series of public lectures on the theme 'The Aims of Education: the Philosophic Approach'. The lectures were given at the University in the Spring Term of 1961 and the texts of five of them are now printed in this volume. The sixth was a summing-up of the series by Lord James of Rusholme and it is regretted that (through no fault of Lord James) it has not proved possible to include it. However, a sixth paper, by Professor Peters, has been included. Professor Peters was asked to give a lecture in the series but, as he was visiting the U.S.A., was unable to do so; he kindly offered to provide a contribution to this volume, however. The lectures are not printed quite in the order they were given; Mr. MacIntyre's, Mr. Wilson's and Mr. Hare's papers are related in some ways and therefore follow one another in the first half of the book; while it seemed appropriate to end with Archbishop Beck's statement of the all-embracing system of St. Thomas and the Neo-Thomists.

The contributors were free to choose their own subjects, within the general field of the 'aims of education' (except that the editor was asked to speak on Dewey) and therefore the reader must not expect to find one theme running through the book, as is usual in collections of this kind. And yet the lectures are not as disparate as they might appear at first sight. This is partly because the first three contributions are closely connected. MacIntyre gives us an analysis of the ills of our society and sees no hope for us unless our children are trained in a new way to think rationally and critically. Although Wilson's theme is a consideration of the nature of, and the struggle against, indoctrination, he too is pessimistic about our society and calls for rationality in our teaching. Hare decided to speak on the same theme as Wilson, after reading the latter's script, and though he brings a new look at the subject, to be expected from a distinguished moral philosopher, the two articles have to be read together, to get the fullest understanding. There are two further aspects, one of content and one of method, which bring some unity to the book. The first is that every lecturer puts forward as his chief aim of education the development of rationality in children. Perhaps it is a little unfair to state this so categorically of Archbishop Beck, for whom the aim of education is the all-round 'making of persons', in a religious context naturally, but all he says emphasizes the importance of rationality, e.g. Neo-Thomism 'lives by reason'; 'it provides a rational account of man'. The other five bring out this principle explicitly. The second point is that most of the contributors think it an essential of philosophic method to make distinctions between, and to analyse, concepts. MacIntyre makes a distinction between ultimate and utilitarian morality and analyses the concept of 'desires', amongst others. Wilson points to the widely accepted distinctions in modern philosophy between the status of scientific, metaphysical and ethical statements, and analyses the concept of indoctrination. Hare carries further the analysis of indoctrination and brings out those characteristics of moral words developed in detail in his recent book.[1] Peters elucidates the problems connected with the concept of 'mental health'. This approach is to be expected

[1] R. M. Hare, *Freedom and Reason*, Oxford, 1963.

in four writers noted for their work in philosophy or philosophy of education, but it is still comparatively rare in
British educational writings. Archbishop Beck is also aware of
the importance of language and he analyses concepts such as
the 'nature of man', but it must be admitted that, by virtue
of his subject, with its long history, he is more in the great
tradition of metaphysical, speculative philosophy (which is
what the ordinary reader expects philosophy to be); he is
also our only writer to show links with the Christian
existentialism (e.g. in his emphasis on the care of 'persons'
and the importance of individual choice) which has proved
acceptable to many educationists in this country.

As books like this are so often read by students training to
be teachers and, more particularly, by their tutors, who have
to teach the theory of education, something should perhaps
be said about the subject called the aims, principles or philosophy of education and the place of these lectures in it.
Clearly there is such a subject, though there is disagreement
about what it should be called and what it should include.
Peters thinks it inappropriate to talk of aims in education, as
the so-called 'aims' are 'neither goals nor . . . end-products',
but are 'ways of talking about doing some things rather than
others and doing them in a certain manner' or they are
'principles implicit in different manners of proceeding or
producing'.[1] As for philosophy of education, there is probably some agreement that the title should not be used unless
the course includes, in O'Connor's words, 'those problems
of philosophy that are of direct relevance to educational
theory'.[2] Few would accept Morris's judgment that 'there is
no such subject as philosophy of education'; that there is

[1] R. S. Peters, *Authority, Responsibility and Education*, London, Allen
& Unwin, 1959, pp. 86, 87.

[2] D. J. O'Connor, *Introduction to the Philosophy of Education*, London,
Routledge & Kegan Paul, 1957, p. 14.

only philosophy, which 'has little use either in education or any other field'; 'the activity of philosophizing can only be recommended as of ultimate value in itself'.[1] As for content, few would wish to limit it to the 'logical distinctions' and 'multifarious workings of language', advocated by O'Connor; most would want to include some of the traditional problems of philosophy, though we might not attain to Harrison's ideal—'stringently self-critical and logically consistent thinking about values, the self, truth, existence, reality, purpose, that irresistibly reveals the logical and moral dependence on it of educational concepts and practices'.[2] Harrison is unduly harsh on books of what he calls 'reflections' on education, which are often the *obiter dicta* of considerable philosophers, like Whitehead's *Aims of Education*, and therefore seminal books, but he is surely right in believing that some stringent thinking about philosophical problems is central to a course in philosophy of education. One wishes to attain many purposes, whatever the name of the course which will consider educational values. First, students expect from philosophy some rational argument about the basic problems of existence; 'l'homme, c'est une passion inutile', says Sartre, and this colourful metaphor sums up the sort of problem they want to hear about; nor is there any reason for denying it to them, in spite of the gaseous clouds of platitude and lay sermonizing that have long surrounded it. Secondly, they do not expect, but they need to acquire, the tools of logical and linguistic analysis and a knowledge of logical distinctions between types of statements and, as this can be an arid task, it is best approached through a study of ethics, which are central to the

[1] C. Morris, *The Role of 'Philosophy of Education'*, University of Leeds, Institute of Education Bulletin, 1962, no. 39.

[2] J. L. Harrison, 'Towards Philosophy of Education', *Educ. for Teaching*, 1962, 59, 13–18.

educator's task, and an analysis of the concepts without which one cannot talk about education at all, such as authority, freedom, determinism, culture, democracy, intelligence and motivation. Thirdly they need an education of the emotions, so that thinking can be accompanied by convictions, and that sensitiveness and idealism can be developed. These aims are not attained independently. A study of the educational great books, the *Republic* and *Culture and Anarchy*, for example, and/or a study of literature, like Wordsworth's *Prelude*, can help in all three areas, if conducted by a teacher who has profited from the books himself and who cares for them. Philosophizing of this kind needs to be supplemented by a course in the principles of education, where a study is made of the psychology and sociology relevant to educational values, where teaching experiences, curricula and organization are thought about and the blue-books discussed; some of this is done, but there is never enough time.

If this line of thought is at all acceptable, it will be seen that the lectures in this volume, if they are considered good in themselves, can make a useful contribution in a philosophy of education course. They deal philosophically with problems which are important in education, and some of them are models of how analysis can be carried out. They are also written to convince, to support ideals which the authors consider worth while; this will be another answer to those who dismiss analysis as negative or irresponsible.

I

AGAINST UTILITARIANISM

by
A. C. MacINTYRE

WHEN I reflect on the doom-laden argument which I am going to present, I fear that I may seem rather like George Fox crying 'Woe to the bloody city of Lichfield!'; although Fox, of course, followed up his denunciation by a constructive message and this I shall conspicuously fail to do. The reason for my failure to be constructive will be very simple. I shall argue that the moral content of our educational system is simply a reflection of the moral content of our society. And so the task of the educator is to attempt to stand against a current which will in fact probably overwhelm him. What strikes me most basically and most finally about our society is its domination by the concept of 'getting on'. One gets on from one stage to the next on an endless conveyor belt. One goes to a primary school in order to pass the eleven plus in order to go to a grammar school in order to go to a university in order to get a degree in order to get a job in order to rise in one's profession in order to get a pension. And those who have fallen out are not people who have found a true end; they are mostly people who have got off, or been pushed off, the conveyor belt. Last year a student whom I knew well had a breakdown as a result of taking seriously the question, 'What am I studying for?' The chain of reasons had no ending.

The failure of both our society and our education lies in

I

its inability to discover ends, to discover purposes which can furnish a sufficient reason for our activities and so render these activities reasonable and satisfying. The root of this failure lies deep in our whole form of social life, a form made articulate and self-conscious in utilitarian moral and political theory. The reason why utilitarianism dominates us is that it provides us with our only public criterion for securing agreement on moral and political questions. We have in our society two sharply contrasting moralities. On the one hand there is the morality of absolute principles. On all sorts of matters we invoke sharply contrasting moral principles: we believe that the H-Bomb is a weapon which ought never to be used in any circumstances *or* that any weapon is legitimate against Communism; we believe that art ought to be socially committed *or* that it should be an entertainment and an escape; we believe that sexuality is a danger to social order and needs restraint *or* that it can be a supreme liberation of human relationship. But on all these matters where moral principles confront one another we have no recognized method for coming to a decision. We treat it as an ultimate of moral reasoning that such disagreements cannot be settled. Precisely because they are disagreements on matters of first principle, no more fundamental principles can be invoked as a court of appeal. But lacking agreement on absolute principles we fall back on our second morality, utilitarianism. For the absolute morality of principles prohibits or enjoins any action of some particular kind. But utilitarianism does not enjoin the performance or non-performance of any specific type of action. It enjoins the performance of any action whatsoever whose consequences will produce the greatest human welfare. Any action, therefore, so it appears, can be brought before the bar of utility. Here is an apparently unitary criterion to settle public disagreements. No matter how ultimate our disagreements on

2

absolute principle, the very continued existence of a co-herent form of social life presupposes an agreement in practice. So the need to continually secure such agreement leads to a continual growth in influence of utilitarianism.

The utilitarian criterion comes before us in many guises. 'Welfare', 'the public interest', 'the interest of the com-munity'—all these phrases suggest a public and socially accepted criterion of action, extrinsic to the action itself, used to judge effects and consequences. In the care to look for the effects of policy, in the suggestion of the community having an interest, in the very vagueness of such expressions as 'welfare' and 'interest' we catch the authentic note of utility. Such phrases are exceptionally liable to occur in educational pronouncements. It is easy to see why they are bound to be influential. Both in the public and private educational sectors we depend upon securing substantial agreement as to the system from those in authority. And since therefore it is the public criteria by which the system has to be evaluated, the public criteria shape the system. Individual schoolmasters or educational administrators may invoke their own principles in their practice; but the form of the school, the curriculum, the goals, these are and must be publicly settled. So they are bound to fall victims to utilitarianism. But why *victims*? What is it in utilitarianism which menaces and threatens?

The elements of utilitarianism upon which I wish to focus attention are, as I have already stated, three-fold. There is first of all the means–end view of human action. We evalu-ate an action by its consequences. The action is a means to something beyond itself. Secondly we evaluate consequences by assessing satisfaction. The assumption is that there is some scale by means of which satisfactions can be measured or at least compared. Thirdly, the position demands that some sense be given to the concept of an overall community of

3

interests, to some notion of 'the greatest happiness of the greatest number'. These positions of utilitarianism have been adequately criticized often enough at the level of philosophical analysis. In so far as I attack them in this paper it is not so much as philosophical theories, but rather as theories embodied in social life, and consequently in educational practice.

What does it mean to speak of a theory as embodied in social life? I can bring this out by considering the relationship between the high-minded humanism of Bentham and the elder Mill on the one hand and the mean-spirited attitudes of Gradgrind and Bounderby in *Hard Times* on the other. Any student of Bentham and Mill must surely at first react to Dickens's portrayal of utilitarianism with charges of unfairness. Bentham and Mill neither resembled Dickens's characters themselves nor did their theory in the slightest degree recommend that people should become like this. And yet Dickens is not unfair. For what Gradgrind and Bounderby are is what utilitarianism had to become when embodied as a belief in the particular social structure which is early industrial capitalism. Utilitarianism is necessarily interpreted in terms of the dominant beliefs and attitudes. Those beliefs are the political economist's faith in a harmony of competing interests, in which the maximization of individual profit leads to a maximization of social well-being. The calculations of action are the calculations of double-entry. Any aspect of life which escapes the calculus escapes the primary consciousness of rational social life. It appears secondary and accidental. And so most ordinary human motives appear secondary and accidental.

What Dickens therefore exposes is the inadequacy of the theory of motives in utilitarianism. But he does so, and is only able to do so, because he stands outside the society whose theory utilitarianism has become. This is important, since it can be a feature of such theories, which are embodied in social life, to become self-confirming. Belief in them sometimes provides the very evidence which appears to confirm them. So if only enough of the Gradgrinds and Bounderbys had adopted utilitarianism and acted on it, their expectations of others around them would have been continuously confirmed. It is the inability of most people to in fact become utilitarians in the *Hard Times* sense that makes the criticism of the system comparatively easy. For it is easy to get outside the system, as Dickens and most of the characters in *Hard Times* are outside it.

What does Dickens contrast with the test of utility? The kind of life that is not a means to any end: activity which finds a purpose within itself, and not in any further end which it may happen to serve. This contrast comes out very well in the terrifying school-room scene where the activity of the horse-riders is contrasted with the abstract knowledge of horses:

'Girl number twenty,' said Mr. Gradgrind, squarely pointing with his square forefinger. 'I don't know that girl. Who is that girl?' 'Sissy Jupe, sir,' explained number twenty, blushing, standing up, and curtsying. 'Sissy is not a name,' said Mr. Gradgrind. 'Don't call yourself Sissy. Call yourself Cecilia.' 'It's father as calls me Sissy, sir,' returned the young girl with a trembling voice, as with another curtsy. 'Then he has no business to do it,' said Mr. Gradgrind. 'Tell him he mustn't. Cecilia Jupe. Let me see. What is your father?' 'He belongs to the horse riding, if you please, sir.' Mr. Gradgrind frowned, and waved off the objectionable calling with his hand. 'We don't want to know anything about that here. You mustn't tell us about that here. Your father breaks horses, don't he?' 'If you please, sir, when they can get any to break, they do break horses in the ring, sir.' 'You mustn't tell us about the ring here. Very well, then. Describe your father as a horse-breaker. He doctors sick horses, I dare say?' 'Oh, yes, sir!' 'Very well, then. He is a veterinary surgeon, a farrier, and horse-breaker. Give me your definition of a horse.' (Sissy Jupe thrown into the greatest alarm by this demand.) 'Girl number twenty unable to define a horse!' said Mr. Gradgrind, for the general benefit of all the little pitchers. 'Girl number twenty possessed of no facts in reference to one of the commonest animals! Some boy's definition of a horse. Bitzer, yours.'

And when Bitzer replies it is to provide a definition that has nothing to do with an ability to handle horses. What Bitzer provides is not a living skill, but dead knowledge.

'Quadruped. Graminivorous. Forty teeth, namely, twenty-four grinders, four eye-teeth, and twelve incisive. Sheds coat in the spring; in marshy countries, sheds hoofs too. Hoofs hard, but requiring to be shod with iron. Age known by marks in mouth.'

A quotation like this which ties us down to a specific situation raises in a sharp form the question of whether Dickens's critique of utilitarianism really can be carried over into contemporary terms. The sequence of argument in the attempt to do this will be as follows. First I shall try to describe those features of contemporary society which exemplify utilitarianism. Then I shall look at the type of character produced by this society. And thirdly I shall ask what role contemporary education plays so that it is the means whereby this specific kind of society produces this specific kind of character.

To turn then to the structure of society: most of those who pass through our educational system will pass into the service of great bureaucracies, whether those of private industry or those of the State. Such bureaucracies are essentially machine-like structures in which each man's work has a function only in serving some end beyond itself elsewhere in the machine. The means–end concept of activity is built into this functional view of work. Automation signifies the replacement of human links by electronic links. Thus the work done serves no purpose which is the purpose of the man who works. His relationship to his own work is dominated by the means–end model in another way too. A man works as a means for the end of leisure. The indulging of leisure as the end of life has already leapt out of the advertisements into the magazine pages, out of the magazine pages into the quality Sunday newspaper supplements. The paradox is that work still seems to have a fundamental importance, while leisure seems comparatively trivial. So that a sense is engendered that the important is being treated as a means to the trivial.

The means–end picture is read in contemporary terms as one in which production is the means, consumption the end. So real human satisfaction belongs to the realm of consumption. The criterion of production is efficiency, for production is only a means. But the terrifying fact is that consumption presently too becomes a means. I think of the American advertising executive who defined his job as being not to give the public what they wanted, but to persuade the public that they wanted what they were going to be given. The weakness of our social theory over this concept of wanting is at least two-fold. First we have two incompatible pictures of wanting. On the one hand we think of wants and likes and tastes as if they were simple, biologically given, indubitable. The boast of the defenders of commercial television, that the public ought to be given what it wants, presupposes that there just *is* that which the public wants. The use of surveys in market research presupposes that people know what they want with the same kind of clarity with which Descartes supposed us to be acquainted with the furniture of our minds. But at the same time nobody knows better than those who control advertising, television and social surveys that desires and tastes are not simple, given, indubitable entities. They have to be and always can be solicited. They do not exist in a vacuum waiting for an object. What we desire depends entirely on what objects of desire have been and are presented to us. *We learn* to want things. Our desires have a history and not just a biological natural history, but a rational, social history of intelligible response to what we are offered. A desire is often more like an answer to a question than it is to a reflex physical movement provoked by a stimulus. Yet those who recognize this are too apt to suppose that desires are just waiting to be elicited and moulded. We are confronted by those who want to give the public what the public wants, on the one hand, and those who want to give the public what they want the public to want, on the other hand. What is lost in this is the concept of the creation of autonomous critical taste, of people who can defend themselves against both the advertisers and the educators, both I.T.V. and B.B.C.

At this point, our failure to clarify the concept of desire fades into our failure to provide a critique of desires and satisfactions. This failure has haunted utilitarianism ever since J. S. Mill's adolescent nervous breakdown. J. S. Mill's own qualitative view of pleasure is notoriously open to attacks almost as devastating as those directed against the quantitative view held by Bentham and by his father. Once more we are left with just what enables the social system to make of us its victims. The utilitarian view that the end of our activity is to satisfy our wants and the utilitarian failure to provide a critique of wanting makes desire apparently indefinitely malleable. And it is in the light of desire thus conceived that consumption is turned from an end into a means. The original picture of the consumer in the market creating demand (inadequate as this was anyway) is transformed into a picture of a producer who creates not only his goods, but also, by means of advertising, the consumer whom he needs for his market. The production of consumption is as much a mark of our society as the consumption

8

of what is produced. Hence each becomes a means to the other and we find once more a chain of activity in which everything is done for the sake of something else and nothing for its own sake.

This autonomous social process in which we are caught up inevitably arranges human beings according to their function; it also inevitably arranges them hierarchically. This follows from the causal means–end model. Since the process is a causal chain, there must be some who can see further along the chain than others. Some mind the levers of social change, some pull them. And at either end of the scale there are those who decide which levers are to be pulled and those who simply *are* levers. This causal, manipulative view of human change belongs essentially to our modern world. It is post-Christian; it belongs to a world where the images of the lever and the machine dominate. But it belongs also and thereby to a world where change in the human realm is assimilated to changing the face of nature. Its philosophical classics range on either side of the utilitarianism of Bentham and Mill towards De La Mettrie's *L'Homme Machine* in the one direction and Robert Owen's *A New View of Society* on the other. The mention of Owen is important in this context because it warns us that good intentions are of no avail against either a misdirected social order or conceptual confusions. (And perhaps it is clear by now that I think that a misdirected social order and conceptual confusions have intimate connexions.) But Owen is specially important because it was against Owen's view that 'the character of man is without a single exception always formed for him' that Marx directed his argument that such a view is bound to be hierarchical.

The materialist doctrine [wrote Marx in his IIIrd Thesis on Feuerbach] that men are products of circumstances and upbringing,

9

and that, therefore, changed men are products of other circumstances and changed upbringing, forgets that it is men
that change circumstances and that the educator must himself be
educated. Hence this doctrine necessarily arrives at dividing
society into two parts of which one is superior to society (in
Robert Owen, for example).

This distinction between those who do good and those on
whom good is inflicted is obvious at every point in our
society. The fact of hierarchy and inequality could scarcely
be at issue. But it is accompanied by a feature which Marx
did not foresee. Marx foresaw the depersonalization of our
life, but not its repersonalization.

Just as in the society of Gradgrind and Bounderby certain
motives were obscured from view without thereby ceasing
to be motives, so in our society all sorts of motives have
become marginal, are thrust back into the obscurity of
private life. It is into the oasis of private life that art, sexuality and all that is deeply personal are extruded. Consider
the warped character of the defence in the *Lady Chatterley*
case. I want to take an apparently eccentric view of this
book, holding neither with some of the defence witnesses
that the book eulogizes a successful human relationship with
complete literary success nor with Dr. Leavis that the book
eulogizes such a relationship, but is a literary failure. Only
one commentator on the trial reminded us that Lawrence
used the word 'tragedy' of his book; that Lawrence saw
Constance Chatterley and Mellors doing the best they
could in a society whose best is essentially a poor one.
But this could not be said in the court case (and if others
disagree with Lawrence about his book I hope they will
allow that even if what he said of it were true, it still
would not have been mentioned in court) because it would
have involved the claim that the book was great art *because*
socially subversive. For Lawrence's critique of the ugliness

of industrial society is essentially pointing to a lack of certain human motives in public social life, and to the way in which those same motives are crippled in private life by the limits public life sets to them.

Yet the personal returns to public life in ways that make the personal too into a means, an instrument. I refer to the way in which those human relationships which ought to be an end in themselves are used to transfer the affections and emotions of human beings to the bureaucracies which imprison them. This is the final obliteration of ends, for the satisfaction of desire which was the end utilitarianism proposed is thus transferred by means of the confusion of our concepts and the weakness of our standards into something which helps us to love Big Brother. Orwell's *1984* is a dangerous book. It makes us believe that *Big Brother* will seem like a tyrant. In fact he will seem like a brother and a friend.

The group [wrote William H. Whyte in *The Organisation Man*] is tyrant; so also is it a friend, and it is *both at once*. The two qualities cannot easily be separated, for what gives the group power over men is the same cohesion that gives it warmth. This is the duality that confuses choice.

What does this kind of social system do to individual character? We see an extension of the bureaucratic mind from the administrative order of the state into every field. No essential differences at this social level appear to divide public corporations from private. About the old public corporations Max Weber wrote:

. . . It is horrible to think that the world could one day be filled with nothing but those little cogs, little men clinging to little jobs and striving towards bigger ones—a state of affairs which is to be seen once more, as in the Egyptian records, playing an ever-increasing part in the spirit of our present administrative system. . . .

The word 'cog' is the only unfortunate one in this passage; for by presenting only the vanishing point of the process in which personality is finally submerged, it obscures the stages by which character deteriorates. The first of these stages is that in which we accept the eighteenth-century, materialist, Owenite picture quite at its face value. There are educators, leaders, moulders on the one side and on the other masses to be moulded, educated, led. It does not matter whom we pick for the role of educator and leader. What does matter is the antithesis of the activity of the leader and of the passivity of the led. The *locus classicus* of the character involved is D. H. Lawrence's portrayal of the character of Gerald in *Women in Love*:

He pushed slowly in his motor-car through the little market-top on Friday nights in Beldover, through a solid mass of human beings that were making their purchases and doing their weekly spending. They were all subordinate to him. They were ugly and uncouth, but they were his instruments. He was the God of the machine. They made way for his motor-car automatically, slowly.

He did not care whether they made way with alacrity, or grudgingly. He did not care what they thought of him. His vision had suddenly crystallized. Suddenly he had conceived the pure instrumentality of mankind. There had been so much humanitarianism, so much talk of sufferings and feelings. It was ridiculous. The sufferings and feelings of individuals did not matter in the least. They were mere conditions, like the weather. What mattered was the pure instrumentality of the individual. As a man as of a knife: does it cut well? Nothing else mattered.

Everything in the world has its function, and is good or not good in so far as it fulfils this function more or less perfectly. Was a miner a good miner? Then he was complete. Was a manager a good manager? That was enough. Gerald himself, who was responsible for all this industry, was he a good director? If he were he had fulfilled his life. The rest was by-play.

The contemporary Gerald would take more account of

sufferings and feelings; he would hand them out to his personnel managers in order that sufferings and feelings too might be made into instruments. Moreover the contemporary Gerald would be less of an individual, more of a collective will. He would be a member of many committees in which his own instrumentality would be put to the service of the corporation. Gerald is already directionless, without true ends. When the two Brangwen sisters discuss him in the novel, Ursula says:

'. . . He'll have to die soon, when he's made every possible improvement, and there will be nothing more to improve. He's got go, anyhow.'

'Certainly, he's got go,' said Gudron. 'In fact I've never seen a man that showed signs of so much. The unfortunate thing is, where does his *go* go to, what becomes of it?'

'Oh I know,' said Ursula. 'It goes in applying the latest appliances.'

Gerald is a distorted human being, in whom thought and feeling have sunk to the level of servants of will, but he still has a human, even if a dying, face. The faceless men of the contemporary corporation are themselves instruments, not by virtue of some act of will of their own, as Gerald is, but by virtue of the structure of the corporation. Hence the difficulty of finding the centres of power in such bodies as I.C.I. or Unilever; in some sense, power has been spread, as compared with the old individualistic, tycoon capitalism. But in a more important sense, everyone is more powerless. The earliest critics of capitalism saw social power as in the hands of 'Them', when it ought to serve 'Us'. But power is now, although it is no nearer 'We', not so much a matter of 'They' as of 'It'.

What happens to 'Us' when they become 'It'? For the answer I want to go to another novel, Alan Sillitoe's *Saturday Night and Sunday Morning*. Why go to novels rather than to pieces of empirical sociological work? Because the sociological investigation is apt to pick out the average, the novelist more likely to pick out the type. The relationship between *Women in Love* and *Saturday Night and Sunday Morning* is that both concern themselves (among other things) with what happens to the energy of a type of individual under given social conditions. Gerald's energy is channelled by acts of will into purposeless activity. Arthur's energy, in Sillitoe's novel, is never used up at all by the purposeless work of mass production at the bicycle factory. The hedonism which runs out into promiscuity, drinking and fighting has enormous vitality because no other constructive ends are offered to Arthur's energy. Yet none of the ends which his hedonism can discover is a true human end, in the sense that his energy can really inform it. Breaking out and feeling frustrated are the poles between which he oscillates. When marriage finally comes upon the scene, it is not as a solution to his problems, but as a way of settling down without solving them. And inside our social framework Arthur's problems necessarily go unresolved. In this sort of society why is anybody surprised at delinquency?

The last stage of all in the shaping of character to fit a society without ends is that in which we moralize the necessary into the ideal. It is tempting, when no activity is offered as its own justification, to say, 'Mine not to reason why. Mine simply to do what lies to hand and to ask no questions about ulterior justification.' From this sort of utterance arises a new and impoverished form of the morality of 'My Station and Its Duty'. Hegel described this morality of doing what lies to hand and making a virtue of not inquiring any further, 'the Spiritual Zoo'. He chose this title presumably because it is the morality of those who live in separate cages and choose not to ask why there are bars or what lies outside them. His full title for it is 'the spiritual

Zoo and Humbug, or the Affair-on-hand itself'. The individual absorbs himself, is swallowed into the given task. What the final outcome is he ignores. This is humbug because it involves the individual in deception both of others and of himself as to his willing complicity in his own victimization by the system. But this point, at which the ultimate degradation of the individual by the system appears to have been reached, reveals in very Hegelian fashion the first ray of light. For if the individual can be willing accomplice in his own enslavement, then he can also not be such an accomplice. But what he can do to avoid this we must delay asking, in order to see how our educational system reflects and endorses our social system.

I have said of the latter that its treatment of men is functional and hierarchical; that no adequate or relevant purpose or ends can be discovered in it; that such ends as men do discover belong to motives which our public life relegates to private obscurity; and that it finally breeds theories to justify its own existence—though this last point I have only touched on briefly. Each of these aspects in turn appears in our educational system. It is clearly functional and hierarchical. The selection methods throw their shadows back into the earliest years of a child's schooling. You are graded by ability and ability is understood functionally. Our educational system, like our social system, is a matter of grooves and ladders. Of grooves because the route the individual takes is determined by factors largely beyond the individual's control. He is sorted out by the luck of the draw in terms of geographical situation, and local authority policies, and in so far as his conscious effort is involved it is in climbing the appropriate ladder to the appropriate rung —and no further. Everything is dominated from the top, by the weight of the Oxford and Cambridge Open Scholarship System.

At the same time ends disappear. The universities do what they do partly because of what the schools do. And the schools do what they do partly because of what the universities do. Each has the other as an alibi. When forced back on justification as to ends, it becomes clear that such ends as our educational system serves are of two kinds. On the one hand they are the ends of practical utility imposed from the outside. Private industry and government need scientists and technologists, administrators and teachers. The educational system provides them. It is quite clear that the only reason why the present university expansion programme in faculties of science and technology has the character it has is because of outside demand. But what about the faculty of arts? Everybody who has worked in a faculty of arts knows two things: that the firmest and most easily usable criterion of what ought to be done is what has been done; and that the hard, verifiable, examinable fact, is always an odds-on favourite when competing with the practice of critical discrimination. It is not of course that in our educational system we neglect the practice of criticism. We do it extremes of violence. Consider for instance what happens to hundreds of general degree standard students in modern universities. They do not know their English literature; they may be profoundly ignorant of Shakespeare. Their grasp of the foreign language which they are studying is imperfect. But they are expected in examinations and essays to express critical opinions on works in those languages of which they are not fully master. The result of course is, as everybody knows, that they feed back at third-hand critical opinions which were second-hand when they received them. Now these people, the general degree students, matter profoundly. They are a potentially articulate public opinion. Yet a good deal is done in practice to cultivate among them the belief that matters of value are arbitrary and conventional.

16

So the university student is presented with a situation in which the ends that dictated his course of study are either imposed from outside or are ends about which his own teachers seem to be unclear and uncertain. And so everything he does seems to be a means to an end which never appears. And to the extent that the university dominates the grammar schools, and the grammar schools dominate the rest, the whole educational system is coloured by this.

Moreover once again the discovery of purposes often belongs to a private area of life unrecognized by the system. I think here of the extraordinary vitality of youth culture, of the autonomy of present-day adolescents in shaping their own lives. The pathetic attempts of the system to come to terms with this (and once again a novel, Colin MacInnes's *Absolute Beginners*, is the best introduction) are reflected not in the silly, condemnatory utterances of the hostile, but in the attempts to understand, to patronize, to annex, of the well-meaning. Everyone must have read those terrible autobiographical accounts of journeys into the teen-age jungle taken by the anthropologists of the *Observer*. And always they get it just that little bit wrong. Of course, the adolescent market is exploited. But the very patronage from the outside reveals curiously often how much it is the young who act, the middle-aged who are the spectators.

The last way in which the educational system reflects the social system is in the growth of justificatory theories. I want here to look at just one of the analyses of the contemporary situation against which a serious question-mark needs to be placed. It is the theory for which Michael Young has popularized the term 'meritocracy'. This is the view that the present hierarchical educational system is justified, because human beings really are divided into 'natural kinds' by ability. So there are those who are best fitted to rule, those who are best fitted to be ruled, and the rest of us, the

c

non-commissioned officers of the provincial universities, the teaching profession and the like, somewhere in between. The trouble with this theory is that it is self-confirming to an entirely unknown extent. What we do know is that people very often behave according to our expectation of them. To make it clear to someone that he is expected to behave in a particular way is often a causally effective method of eliciting the expected behaviour. In our society, divided as it is along class-lines which correspond roughly to the divisions in our schools, people are presented from a very early age with expectation as to how they will behave. There are 'A' stream people, 'B' stream people, and 'C' stream people: so the story is told to people again and again. We ought not therefore be surprised that they start behaving as if this were true. And by so doing they make the theory of meritocracy appear to be confirmed. But what appeared to confirm the theory was the effect of belief in it. And so the theory is not really confirmed at all. (It is interesting here to note that when philosophy is taught to students in Colleges of Art, philosophy being a subject against which people have not been conditioned at school and the students coming from anything from secondary modern schools to university scholarship sixth forms, there appears to be no correlation between educational background and ability.)

So far then the educational system's characteristic vices are those of the social system. But here another matter arises. The view that what we do must always be a means to an end contradicts the very nature of rational inquiry. Professor John Anderson has written:

it may be pointed out that the classical and the utilitarian views of education are distinguished as employing intrinsic and extrinsic criteria, the one considering education in its own character, as the development of thinking or criticism, the other considering it in its contribution to something else, subordinating it in this way

18

to the non-educational and running the greatest risk of distorting its character. For clearly there can be no subject or field of study which is utilitarian in itself, whose character resides in what it produces or helps to produce, and this applies as much to science as to any other study; its intrinsic character, taken as the search for laws, the study of the ways of working of actual things, has no reference to the turning of its findings to 'practical' account.

Professor Anderson's remarks provide what I take to be the key in educational theory. Our aim ought to be to help people to discover activities whose ends are not outside themselves; and it happens to be of the nature of all intellectual inquiry that in and for itself it provides just such activity. The critical ability which ought to be the fruit of education serves nothing directly except for itself, no one except those who exercise it.

About critical ability I want to stress three things. First it is the antithesis of that acceptance of wants, tastes and prejudices as given facts which so disfigures our society. For critical activity involves the testing of any claim to knowledge or understanding at the bar of some impersonal, rational criterion. The difference between Socrates and the pre-Socratics lies precisely in the demand for and the attempt to formulate such a criterion. Secondly, critical ability is something which each has to acquire for himself. Nobody else can be critical on my behalf. So the test of whether a student has really grasped a piece of knowledge is whether he can defend it before such a criterion. And this means that to understand is never to be able merely to produce the conclusion without the premises, the finished end-product of knowledge without the way it was arrived at. Every acquisition of knowledge relives a past discovery. Thirdly, to have seen this is to see that the element of universality in all criticism is perfectly compatible with specialization. The unity of criticism lies in the fact that all understanding and all knowledge is a matter of concepts and to that degree philosophical; and that all understanding and all knowledge is acquired as dependent upon its own past intellectual background and is to that degree historical. But the unity of criticism, such as it is, in philosophy, history and science does not demand that critical ability has to be shown in every field. Rather it is the case that only in concrete examples worked out in depth can criticism flourish. Thus academic specialization may be justified for its own sake and is not merely a symptom of the functional view of man in society.

But there is something more important still about critical activity. It is not the activity of isolated individuals. It is always exercised inside an academic tradition which is the tradition of some particular society. Unless critical standards claim social recognition, criticism is untrue to its own claims to universal allegiance. But a condition of this is precisely the refusal to make criticism the prerogative of an elite. For to create an elite is to allow a debasement of standards for everyone else. And to allow this is to make criticism the instrument of one part of society against the other. But to claim such a prerogative for some special class is precisely to restrict the moral openness which critical activity requires. We are all equal before the impersonal standards of reason and there is no brother of whom we are not the keeper. Thus intellectual standards and democratic community need each other.

There is a bad conception of popular culture which is sometimes invoked by those who forget this. On this conception there are two cultures, the literate culture of the elite and the non-literate culture of the masses. But all culture which fosters critical activity must accept the standards of literacy. A dangerous and misleading book here is Richard Hoggart's *The Uses of Literacy*. For Hoggart here ascribes the positive values of working-class life to pre-literate forms of communal living and the decline of values to literacy. But in fact the working-class whose life Hoggart depicts did not spring intellectually virgin from the rural landscape into industrial society. Even those who came more recently from the countryside inherited a tradition embodied in habits of mind and ways of acting which was formed in the Chartist movement and in the early Trade Unions. And into the formation of this tradition there went an immense amount of reading. When Thomas Cooper joined the Leicester Chartists in 1841, he helped to teach in the adult Sunday school they founded where the classes were called the William Cobbett class, the Tom Paine class, the George Washington class, the John Bunyan class and so on. It was a literate working-class tradition that was debased by illiteracy and not *vice versa*.

I hope it is clear from all this that the values of rational, critical inquiry seem to me to stand in the sharpest contrast to the prevailing social values. The task of education is to strengthen the one and weaken the other. Above all the task of education is to teach the value of activity done for its own sake. And this will only be partially done if it is restricted to rational inquiry in the narrower sense; for rational inquiry in the narrower sense will not remain rational. Unless the feelings too are sifted and criticized, the feelings are simply handed over to unreason. We have to allow those whom we teach to remake themselves through their activity. And if we do this, we shall be educating those who may in the end help to remake society itself. For critical inquiry is not utilitarian; it is not functional; it is not hierarchical; it demands independence of mind and feeling; it demands all that our society tends to deny us. Above all critical inquiry is not an academic retreat; for its maintenance presupposes rebuilding a particular kind of community.

Finally, a last look in either direction: at what I am against in this lecture and what I am for. What I am against is embodied dramatically in two recent political narratives. The first is the story of the atomic scientists in Robert Jungk's *Brighter Than a Thousand Suns*. Here what terrifies is the way in which first-rate minds uncritically went from stage to stage in the manufacture of the first nuclear weapons without ever raising the question of what they were actually doing. Their horrified surprise when they learnt that the end of the process was near, that the bomb which they had made was about to be used, shows what happens when intellectual activity is uncritically subservient to practical ends. The individuals who made the bomb did not will it; it seemed just to have come. And it was used largely because it was there. Or read Sir Anthony Eden's *Memoirs* and see how, where, one might have thought, if a victim of the contemporary meritocratic ideology, that a high I.Q. could not but guarantee intelligence serving worthwhile purposes, there appears instead, in the approach to Suez, a sleepwalker moving with the best of intentions and the highest intelligence unerringly towards disaster. In each case the impersonality of the social order can be seen taking over intelligence and turning it into the instrument which utilitarianism has taught us to believe that it is.

On the other side I have to look back in time. We are too far gone to throw up in our society at present many pure images of what we ought to be and are not. But the concept of activity for its own sake casts a shadow in images as long as there is art. Its finest statement—its last for our society perhaps—is in Yeats. It may be more than poetic coincidence that it is in the poem *Among School Children* that the relation of the agent to his activity is imaged:

> Labour is blossoming or dancing where
> The body is not bruised to pleasure soul,
> Nor beauty born out of its own despair,

Nor blear-eyed wisdom out of midnight oil.
O chestnut tree, great-rooted blossomer,
Are you the leaf, the blossom or the bole?
O body swayed to music, O brightening glance,
How can we know the dancer from the dance?

When for all of our children the relation of the mind to what it grasps can be as that of the dancer to the dance, we shall be living in a form of society in which the argument of this lecture will no longer be relevant.

II

EDUCATION AND INDOCTRINATION

by

JOHN WILSON

QUESTIONS like 'What is education?' or 'What are the aims of education?' are often a mere waste of time, because they are an excuse for the person who answers them to put forward various opinions of his own as if they constituted the only true answer; and as any philosopher will tell you, there cannot be a true answer to such questions, because they are not true questions. 'What is education?' You might be asking for a dictionary definition of the word 'education', or for a sociological account of the causes of existing educational processes, or for someone's opinion about what these processes *ought* to be, or for practically anything. So in Plato's *Republic*, in answer to the question 'What is justice?', Polemarchus gives a dictionary answer ('giving each man his deserts'), Thrasymachus gives a sociologist's answer ('a code of law in the interests of the ruling classes'), and Socrates an answer designed to attach his own ideals to the word 'justice', which he says is 'each man doing his proper job in society'. Compare also three answers to the question 'What is religion?': from a dictionary, 'Belief in the supernatural'; from Marx, 'The opium of the people'; from a Christian, 'Following Jesus Christ'.

But it would be a mistake to write off as useless all general discussion which takes its starting-point from a word like 'education', however imprecise such discussion may be, and however many logical varieties of answers may be given to such general questions. For the most valuable result of such discussion is that, perhaps only half-consciously, we map out the area of meaning of a particular concept, and sketch its logical geography by contrasting it with other concepts, paying attention to borderline cases where we are in doubt, considering model cases which we know to form part of the concept's geography, and so forth. This is not merely an academic exercise, for by it—and by it alone—we come to appreciate certain salient and important features of the general landscape. We begin with nebulous words and concepts like 'education', 'social adjustment', 'self-realization', 'discipline' and so on, and though we do not and cannot end with a single straight answer which magically defines any of these, we do end with something. We find no hidden treasure, because there is none: but we do find certain general principles, hitherto unknown or only half-comprehended, which prove of immense practical value. To take a parallel case, discussions about 'natural rights', 'the state and the individual', 'freedom' and so on in political theory may seem very clumsy and logically muddled, as indeed they are. But they are not a waste of time. By considering actual cases of freedom and oppression, of conflicts between state and individual, of human rights and communal necessity, we come to formulate principles which are important even though they may be imprecise: as, for instance, the principles of liberal democracy on which the western world is based.

One of the concepts which it is most useful to contrast with education is the notion of indoctrination. This is of importance, because we are anxious to establish general principles about *how* and *what* we are to teach children, or how we are to wield educational influence in general: and the word 'indoctrination' represents a nebulous but large area of logical terrain from which we feel, vaguely, that we ought to keep well away. 'Indoctrination' represents, to most of us, something pernicious, though we are not quite sure what: an area whose frontiers, if we only knew where they were, we do not want to cross. Perhaps we may think of education as a country lying between two bordering states: on the left, a state of not bothering enough about children or people, and on the right, a state of bothering too much or bothering in the wrong way—a state of indoctrinating them. Where do the frontiers of this state lie?

The model cases of indoctrination are obvious: brain-washing people to believe in Communism, teaching Christianity by the threat of torture or damnation, forcing people by early training to accept social roles as in Huxley's *Brave New World*. But what is, at bottom, our objection to such cases? Suppose we could teach four-year-old children all their mathematical tables while they were asleep, or by hypnosis? Or suppose that a boy could master A Level physics simply by having an electric charge passed through his brain-cells? Is this indoctrination or not? I want to make it very clear at this point that the answer here is logically arbitrary. We can say yes or no as we choose. The important point is that we should not disapprove of such cases (assuming the hypnopaedia or electric charges had no ill effects, and other things in general being equal): so that, if we still want to keep the word 'indoctrination' as the name of a forbidden area, we shall probably want to say that these cases are not cases of indoctrination.

Then what is the difference between hypnotizing a boy to believe in Communism and hypnotizing him to master A Level physics? Plainly it is not a difference in *method*: it is rather a difference of subject-matter. Consider cases where we would object to hypnotic persuasion: cases of persuasion towards political belief, religious belief, or moral belief. Then consider cases where we would not object: cases of teaching mathematics, Latin grammar, swimming, how to drive a car. What is the root of the distinction here? Is it that political and moral beliefs are closer to the heart of the individual than other beliefs and skills—that we object to deep-level interference of this kind but are prepared to overlook more superficial matters such as mathematics and Latin grammar?

This will not do, as we can see if we look at one more case. Suppose we hypnotized a boy to believe (or alternatively to deny) that there was life on other planets in the universe. We should object to this, even though we might think the issue of little practical importance compared with religious or moral issues. Our objection is surely founded on the fact that whether or not there is life on other planets is an *uncertain question*, that we have no logical right to be sure of the answer. The same applies to the other issues to which we object. Religious, political and moral beliefs are *uncertain*, in a sense in which mathematics and Latin grammar are not uncertain. And for reasons which I will develop later, we object to closing people's minds on uncertain issues.

It is of great importance to see just *how* these beliefs are uncertain. Many people regard their religious and moral beliefs as quite certain, so that it might seem as if we had the right to teach them by hypnosis just like Latin grammar. But faced with the fact that, however strongly convinced people are about these beliefs, nevertheless different people believe different things, we are prepared—with some reluctance—to place them in a special category. If we did not do so, we should leave it open to our religious, political and moral enemies to indoctrinate as well as to ourselves: and after a good deal of blood-stained history, some of us have decided, in some areas of belief at least, to call a truce. These beliefs are uncertain in this sense: that it is not true that any

27

sane and sensible person, when presented with the relevant facts and arguments, would necessarily hold the beliefs. We might put this by saying that there was no *publicly-accepted* evidence for them, evidence which any rational person would regard as sufficient. Thus there are rational people who believe in Communism, Roman Catholicism, and free love, as well as rational people who believe in liberal democracy, some kind of Christian religion and the sexual conventions of the western world. To say that there are not rational people who believe these things is to break the truce and declare war: and by doing so we *ipso facto* declare our opponents to be lunatics and allow ourselves to use any weapon against them. This is to tread precisely on the forbidden ground which we demarcate by the title 'indoctrination'.

If we are to avoid indoctrination, therefore, the beliefs we teach must be rational. They need not be certain in the sense of being 100 per cent proved: it may only be that the general weight of evidence is in their favour. They *may* be certain, or they may be highly probable, or probable, or just likely on the whole. What they *must* be is backed by evidence: and by 'evidence', of course, we must mean publicly-accepted evidence, not simply what sectarians like to consider evidence: otherwise the truce is again broken, since we must then allow anyone to say that there is evidence for any belief whatsoever. All this stands in sharp contrast to beliefs which are held by the majority of any society, or beliefs which we think to be 'good' for children, or beliefs which are traditional, or beliefs which we think help to keep society together. The concept of indoctrination concerns the truth and evidence of beliefs, and our objection to it is basically that in the realm of belief we must put truth, evidence and reality first, and other considerations second.

The importance of evidence implies that we must grade our teaching to fit the logical status of the beliefs which we are putting forward. If they are certain, in the sense that elementary mathematics and Latin grammar are certain, they can be taught as certainties: if they are merely probable, as with some historical interpretations, they must be taught as probabilities: and if they are totally uncertain, they must not be taught at all—at least in the sense that we must not persuade people to adopt them. Obviously, however, there are few 100 per cent certainties, and it would be dangerous to use any method of teaching which did not allow the pupil the chance to reject the belief, either at the time or in the future. No scientific or empirical belief, for instance, can claim absolute certainty. All this further emphasizes the point that, to avoid indoctrination, we must be more concerned with putting forward the evidence for beliefs than with inculcating the beliefs themselves. There are, of course, plenty of cases where the evidence is so obvious and overwhelming that we need spend little time on it: we can again use the examples of mathematics and Latin grammar. But there are plenty of other cases which are not so obvious: and it is these which present us with the practical problems.

We have singled out religious, political and moral beliefs as uncertain, and also quoted the question of whether there is life on other planets as a question whose answer is uncertain. But it is important to see that the former—the metaphysical and moral beliefs—are uncertain in a deeper sense than that in which the answer to any scientific question is uncertain. For with a scientific question we at least know what *sort* of evidence would count towards an acceptable answer: we are agreed in principle about *how* to answer. But with metaphysical and moral questions we are not agreed. We do not know what sort of evidence to look for. 'Is there a God?', 'Is homosexuality wicked?', 'Ought we to have laws against gambling?'—we do not know the answers to these; but, worse, we do not know what sort of evidence to bring forward, or how much weight should be attached to various bits of evidence. Is human suffering evidence against a loving God? Some say yes, some say no. We don't know. We don't even know exactly what is being claimed by such statements as 'There is a God'—exactly what this sort of statement means. Again, is there really such a thing as absolute right and wrong? And what sort of laws are governments entitled to make, anyway? These are complex matters, about which philosophers are still not in agreement. We cannot even be sure that any question of truth, falsehood, or evidence arises at all with metaphysical and moral issues: they may be no more than expressions of foolish desires, matters of taste and prejudice, fond hopes or vain imaginings. We know, of course, that they are important, at least in the sense that a great part of human life is necessarily concerned with them. But we do not know exactly how they are important. We do not know how to tackle them: we can only grope around, trying to remain awake and perceptive, tolerant yet not casual, allowing that we are in the dark and yet continually striving to gain more light. To pretend otherwise is to neglect the immense gulf between the territory of science and common sense on the one hand, and the far more mysterious territory of metaphysics and morals on the other. To put it briefly: we know how to do science, but we do not know how to do metaphysics or morals. I think we should also remain aware of the fact that all this is sufficiently obvious to an intelligent child, though he might not be able to state it clearly.

Many people feel that if we do not teach specific religious, moral and political beliefs, the children are left in an intolerable vacuum. Such people, if they are also aware of the dangers of indoctrination, may think that the best we can do is to display a shop-window of different religious, moral and political wares, demonstrate as many of them as we can, and

allow the children to choose for themselves. This will not
do. First, the wares never vary enough to be interesting:
only safe goods are allowed. Thus, headmasters may demonstrate various views on sexual behaviour to their pupils, but
it is unlikely that their demonstration of the theory of free
love will be more than half-hearted: and similarly the radio
and television may hawk various opinions on religion, but
will be unlikely to give much space to an avowed atheist
(except, of course, on the Third Programme, where it is
reasonably certain that not many people will listen to him).
Secondly, the children are well aware of the prevailing
views about morality and religion, and one of their chief
interests will be the extent to which such views are sensible:
they want to know whether they should yield to social
pressure or withstand it. They do not want to be taken for a
conducted tour round a world curiosity shop; they want to
know whether any of the beliefs are *true*. Thirdly, and most
important of all, it is not at all true that refusal to inculcate
specific beliefs results in a vacuum; and the fact that some
people think it does is a grave symptom of our outlook on
education in general. Children—and adults, for that matter—
want to *communicate*: to form attachments and to form
opinions: not to be left alone. It is failure of communication
which results in a vacuum, in the isolation which is a root-
cause of so many educational and social ills. Nobody, I hope,
will believe that the only form of communication is the
inculcation of beliefs: there is such a thing as rational discussion. The fact that we do not know something is not in
itself a cause of isolation: we can join hands and grope towards an answer together. To pretend that we do know
something, when we do not know it, isolates people far
more: for it turns them away from reality, which is the
only ground on which we can meet and communicate, and
projects them into some form of fantasy-escape from the

31

demands of the real world. Such cowardice never pays in the end.

Few teachers, I think, would want to deny that there is plenty of interest among children in questions of religion, politics and morality: particularly where such questions impinge on their everyday experience—as, for instance, questions of sexual behaviour do. And where there is interest, provided it is not submerged beneath indoctrination, there can be discussion and genuine learning. It is, after all, our children, or their descendants, who are—we hope—going to solve some of the problems which we are now uncertain about: and perhaps the chief reason why we have not solved them already is that all of us hitherto have been crippled at the start by one form or another of indoctrination. If we can give them a clean start, we may work wonders.

I do not pretend that rational communication is not a very difficult matter. For there are a great many forms of inculcating beliefs, a great many forms of indoctrination, other than the overt methods of brain-washing or rubber truncheons. There is the mother who says, 'Of course you can do what you like, dear, but I should be very *sad* to think that my daughter was having an affair with some man': the housemaster who says, 'We have complete religious toleration here, Bloggs, but of course I've always liked to have *Christian* boys as prefects': the school governor who says, 'No political discrimination, of course, Mr. Sloggs, but naturally you'll see that we shall get a bad name if any of the boys do actually become Communists, so perhaps you'd better not teach them about it.' In many cases the indoctrination is more effective if the indoctrinator is loved or admired: it is when the political individual *loves* Big Brother that he really loses his freedom. Amidst all these temptations it is hard to establish a purely rational form of communication: but the difficulty lies in ourselves as teachers, not elsewhere.

Rational communication consists in not putting pressure on the individual in a way which his conscious mind cannot fully resist, in talking in such a way as to draw out the individual's feelings, to make him more conscious, and thus to expand his personality as opposed to contracting or interfering with it. (We might think here of the contrast between the pressure of moralizing, and the drawing out of psychoanalysis.) We present the individual with facts which may help him to form a decision: we try to show him aspects of his own feelings and desires of which he was not fully aware: we clarify for him points of logic and language which may be hindering his intellect from functioning properly. To say that we are here acting as 'teachers' may be misleading: for we are not trying to teach him any particular belief, but trying to help him to reach beliefs for himself.

It should now be clear on what our basic objections to this sort of indoctrination are based. It is not only that we do not want closed minds on open questions, for the sake of social progress merely. It is that we value the human personality, and *do not want it to be diminished*. Our love of freedom and dislike of interference is rooted in the desire to expand each individual to his fullest extent: and to inculcate certainty where there is no real certainty is one form—and a very serious form—of preventing this expansion. Freedom is a necessary condition for individual and social progress, for the expansion and development of a personality or a society. It is not, however, a sufficient condition: we need to add to it by communication, by bringing forward the experiences and methods which enable the structure of personality and belief to be built. Freedom gives us a site to build on: but we also need the raw materials.

Hitherto we have been considering indoctrination in the context of teaching beliefs—and by implication, teaching them by word of mouth to children or adults who are old enough to understand fully what we teach. But the same points hold good in the far wider and more important area of teaching behaviour, and the general upbringing of children who are too young for rational communication as we have so far described it. This area is wider and more important, because a child's early upbringing will largely determine not only his behaviour-patterns but also the general trend and tone of his beliefs. Obviously, if we had considered the essence of indoctrination to consist in certain *methods* of education—for instance, hypnosis as opposed to rational discussion—then we should have had to conclude that the indoctrination of young children was inevitable: for since young children and infants cannot discuss, the methods we use to educate them are bound to resemble hypnosis and brain-washing more than they resemble a democratic exchange of views. But having seen that the criterion of indoctrination depends on the rationality of the *content* of what is taught, rather than the methods, we have now an equally useful principle for early education.

This principle consists in only educating children to adopt behaviour-patterns and to have feelings which are seen by every sane and sensible person to be agreeable and necessary. These behaviour-patterns will be rational, in the sense that they derive from reality rather than from the values, fears, desires or prejudices of individual people. If a child touches the fire, it gets burnt. This is a model example of education: nothing distorts reality here for the child—he simply touches it and it burns him. But of course the workings of reality are sometimes too slow for the child to appreciate: it may not be mentally capable of connecting the unripe apple with the subsequent stomach-ache, the refusal to go to bed with the subsequent bad temper, the stealing of a few sweets in Woolworth's with the subsequent magistrate's court. So adults simplify reality for the child, acting in such a way as to encourage it to behave rationally towards reality and discourage the opposite. This is the proper function of education—for the educator to act as an intermediary between the child and reality, clarifying and interpreting. Indoctrination begins when the behaviour we teach children is behaviour demanded by ourselves and not by reality at all: when we force on the child a particular interpretation of reality which *we* may think good, but which an ancient Greek or a medieval Chinaman or a modern Red Indian would think wicked, absurd or unnecessary.

In the interests of philosophical clarity we ought, perhaps, to remember that, strictly speaking, the mere process of getting someone to *do* something is not indoctrination. If I stop a child from stealing, or carry it upstairs to bed kicking and screaming, this may be force, and it may or may not be right, but it is not indoctrination. Indoctrination creeps in either when I make it do something irrational, or—and this is perhaps more important—when in my endeavour to make it do a rational action, I try to make it believe something irrational. For instance if I say in the imperative mood 'Go to bed!', or just pick it up and take it to bed, I merely compel: but if I say 'If you don't go to bed you'll never grow up a big, strong boy', or 'Aunt Doris won't give you a present for Christmas', or 'God will be very angry', then this is to indoctrinate. To say 'If you insist on sleeping with girls we shall have to expel you, because people don't like schoolboys doing this' is no more than the truth: but to say 'This sort of sex is dirty' or 'This sort of sex isn't the sort of mature, responsible relationship which all the marriage experts and doctors and educationalists like, so it must be bad' is indoctrination. The test, as we have seen, consists of the *content* of what we teach.

It is worth remarking, in this context, that the picture of children entering the world in a state of purity, trailing clouds of glory, and then being corrupted by wicked in-doctrinators is almost certainly a false one. The human situation is tragic, and original sin an incontrovertible fact, in the sense that at a very early age the infant child has met with immense difficulties in facing reality, and has already distorted it into the most fantastic pictures: a harsh fact, basically due to the helplessness of the human offspring when compared with other animals, and to its inability to express its desires and control its environment. This means that we are not so much trying to avoid corrupting the child, as try-ing to educate it *out of* these fantasy-distortions: to bring its wild desires, horrific fears, and hopeless passions into line with reality. Our chief task, therefore, is to avoid bringing our own distortions to bear on the child: for they will only too easily strike a chord in the child's mind. Guilt, irrational fear, tension, anxiety, insecurity and hate are there already. It is our business to bring them into the light and thus dissi-pate them: not to reinforce them by our own hidden feelings.

I am not, of course, saying that our own feelings and desires about children are irrelevant. Some of those feelings are themselves a part of reality, which we are not only entitled but obliged to present to the child: but others are prejudices which are not shared by all rational human beings. For instance, if a child kicks up a row when there are adults in the room who want a quiet conversation, it is plainly right to make him shut up—if necessary by force. The desires of human beings besides itself are a part of reality—perhaps the most important part—which it has to learn to understand. To allow the child to go on making a row in such circumstances is just as much indoctrination as to stop it making a noise in its own play-room, because it presents the child with a false picture—a picture of lunatic adults who are willing to stop talking just because some kid is screaming; and any sensible child knows or at least suspects that this picture *is* false. On the other hand, to object to children being untidy in their own room, or using what *we* choose to call bad language, or engaging in erotic play, is to indoctrinate. There is nothing in reality which we can claim to be interpreting if we make an objection of this kind: we are simply passing on our own misinterpretation.

Naturally problems arise because we are living in an irrational society, as all societies are. There is of course one obvious sense in which the irrational prejudices of a society, both in its beliefs and in its behaviour-patterns, form part of reality. Thus, in one sense it is not in reality true that certain words are, as it were by magic, bad language: but it is true that certain words are 'bad language', in inverted commas, in certain societies: i.e. people in those societies will react to them in a particular way. To some extent one has to compromise with this: if not as regards a child's beliefs, at least as regards its behaviour. It must acquire the habit of a minimum of conformity, even in a wildly irrational society, if it is to survive at all. The worse forms of indoctrination can be avoided, however, if it is made clear to the child that these irrational prejudices are simply awkward features of reality, like fires that burn or mountains that get in the way. So long as the educator does not imply that he is on their side, little damage is done. For example, at the school where I work[1] boys are not allowed to use fish-and-chip shops, or to eat in public. It would take a great deal of argument to convince me that anyone's objections to fish-and-chips, or to eating a chocolate biscuit in the streets, were based on a cool-headed and scientific appreciation of reality, on the basis of which he had made a wise and profound moral judgment. On the other hand, if boys at my school do eat fish-and-chips, tiresome old ladies write letters to the

[1] At the time this lecture was given the author was Second Master at The King's School, Canterbury.

headmaster complaining that boys are not what they were, respectable citizens (who have trout and sauté potatoes in expensive clubs instead) spread the word around that the school is going downhill, and so forth. So I have to stop them doing it. But I do not have to suggest that this is anything more than a tiresome rule made to humour the particular Establishment on which public schools depend for a living. In fact, I rather go out of my way to make this clear: because nobody is going to persuade a sane adolescent that it can be anything else. And since the boys are in favour of the school and appreciate the truth, they generally keep the rules. In other words, where there are irrational prejudices, they must be overtly taught as such, and not taught as sound moral principles.

Just as some people think that to avoid giving what they would call positive instruction about religion and morals leaves children in a vacuum, so it is also thought that to teach young children only rational behaviour-patterns isolates them in the same way. But again, we here forget the possibilities of communication. Throughout the educational process the educator should not act as a moralizer or as an instrument for passing on the prejudices of his society: if he does, he indoctrinates. But that does not mean he is emotionally neutral towards the child. The belief that words like 'logic', 'reason', 'objectivity' and so on go together with words like 'cold', 'unemotional', 'arid', etc. is a silly myth. *Of course* the educator must be on the side of the child, supporting it, loving it, and communicating with it in its learning about reality. His job is to give the child love and to give it clarity: but not the pseudo-love which cannot bear to see the child showing a different set of moral feelings from himself, or the pseudo-clarity which insists on the child sharing his own simplified fantasy-myths which are his travesty of reality.

Having thus sufficiently sketched the concept of indoctrination as a matter of logic and language, we must now turn in a more practical way to particular danger-spots—areas where indoctrination is especially menacing. Most societies, of course, have no end of fun in attacking indoctrination in areas where they do not themselves indoctrinate. Thus, educationalists in our society enjoy themselves in letting off steam about the colour bar and race prejudice, though these are not forms of indoctrination which we normally practise in England. But it is plain enough that it is just those areas where a society indoctrinates that educators—if education is worth anything at all—must be determined to liberate. The danger is worse if the indoctrination is practised by subtle, non-overt methods which form an almost unnoticed part of the warp and woof of society: brain-washing and rubber truncheons may provoke a political reaction, but more skilful inducements can only be countered by those with the intelligence and desire to apprehend and check them. And the danger is worse still if the content of indoctrination distorts important features of the individual's personality. If every child were indoctrinated to stand on its head and repeat 'abracadabra' before breakfast every morning, I doubt whether any serious damage would be done: but if children are taught to regard sex as something to feel guilty about, that is another matter.

No educator can remain neutral in an irrational society, for not to act is as decisive as to act: with children particularly, one cannot avoid adopting some attitude or other. What, then, can be suggested to guide the educator in the task of avoiding indoctrination and equipping his pupils for that same task?

1. First, he must realize his own lack of freedom as an educator. He must appreciate the extent to which education

is dominated by factors which have little to do with rationality: by popular opinion, parental pressure, national demands, and local prejudices: in short, by a social set-up—an Establishment, if you like—which tries to make sure that the irrational prejudices of a society *are* passed on to its children. The expectations of this Establishment often run directly counter to what the educator would like to do if he had a free hand; assuming that the educator is himself rational and emotionally dissociated from the Establishment. The educator must, in other words, identify the opposition before he can begin to fight at all. The fact that the opposition is not, or not always, consciously directed, but is more like an unthinking set of emotional reactions, does not make it less real—or, necessarily, less powerful.

2. Secondly, he must appreciate the general ways in which his society is irrational and hence repressive. In the case of western society, and indeed in most industrial societies, this means that he must be sociologically aware: aware, for instance, that such societies are power-seeking and status-seeking societies largely incapable of spontaneous enjoyment, guilt-ridden in matters of sex and sensual enjoyment generally, lacking in communication and co-operative effort, neurotically isolated, tense and lonely, obsessed by the symbols of prestige and to a great extent incapable of honesty.

3. Thirdly, he must be realistic about the methods of changing society. He must be radical in his idealism, radical in his insistence on testing everything by the standards of rationality, but as wise as a serpent in appreciating what he can do personally. He needs the awareness of the rebel and the political skill of the conformist. To be a Bohemian, a rebel, an angry young man, a sniper at the Establishment, or a cynic, is wholly a waste of time, because it produces no effective results. He should regard himself more as an

espionage agent, a member of a fifth column, in enemy-occupied territory: his position calls for continued devotion to his cause, but also for the ability to survive and operate effectively. Questions of moral integrity, honesty, or overt truthfulness do not arise. We live in a mad world: what counts is not preserving our own integrity, but making the world saner.

All this is particularly important in an age of affluence and apathy. We live in a society whose chief aim is to preserve and if possible expand a technological culture, whose end-product is the private possession of consumer goods. Nearly all questions of government home policy are concerned with this, and nearly all citizens acquiesce in it and indeed insist upon it. The significant alternatives are not choices between Communism and western democracy, Socialism or Conservatism, public service or private profit: they are between a technological and acquisitive culture, as we find it in all industrialized countries, together with all the moral and political values of such a culture, and whatever other kind of culture we have the imagination to think of and the guts to achieve. The success, by its own standards, of tech-nological culture in the western world, in Russia, and to an increasing extent in other countries everywhere, has already resulted in political and moral apathy, the apathy of people who perhaps for the first time in history have been given a reasonable amount of economic and political security. They have not been given a psychological security, however: indeed one might almost think that the former type of security has militated against the latter, and that the removal of the necessity for economic and political struggle has made the individual isolated and neurotic. Driven since the Reformation by a compulsive desire to work and to acquire, and now for the first time presented with more possessions than he knows what to do with, he finds himself lost, without any tribe or community to back him and give him support, and without any capacity for spontaneous and creative enjoyment. Most of his education, remember, has been designed to enable him to keep up with the technology: to find a job which will give him the status and money he expects, and which at the same time will be technologically useful. He has been taught to succeed and to be respectable: and his criteria of success and respectability will be largely defined by the standards of the social class immediately above him. Thus, in so far as there was a working-class culture in any way opposed to or different from the technological culture which we now enjoy, it has been and is being abolished by the absorption of the working-classes into the middle-classes. There is thus no opposition to the technological culture from under-privileged persons, because those who used to be under-privileged have been bribed off— bribed by more consumer goods, and by the chance of rising in society via a grammar school education. The only opposition comes from a number of discontented intellectuals, who write sociological books about it which cut no ice.

In a detribalized society which feels insecure, such as our own society is, indoctrination will generally take the form of pressure towards conformity which is disguised by a pseudo-liberal attitude. A hundred years ago in England, in America and in most other countries, there were in our environment strong, authoritarian features which commanded our allegiance: a patriarchal father, the demands of a naive patriotism, unquestioned belief in moral standards and religious faith. Owing to increased social mobility, these authoritarian features are no longer with us: but it would be a mistake to suppose that we are any more free than we were before. The old men of the tribe now tell a different story: but there are still old men. The stern moralist has been replaced by the kindly but still compulsive modern parent, social worker, or psychologist. We are no longer 'wicked' or 'vicious': but we are 'immature' and 'maladjusted' instead. Because people have not the strength to stand on their own feet, and form their friendships and attachments spontaneously, the need for conformity still exists: indeed it exists more strongly because there is no ready-made framework of attachments which we are compelled to fit into.

This pseudo-liberal indoctrination whose doctrine is adjustment to society and a 'mature' acceptance of social responsibility is a good deal more pernicious than the stern authoritarianism of past ages, because it appears omnipotent, and seems backed by modern psychological science. In fact, of course, we have no clear conception of mental health current in this society which does not involve reference to fitting in with this society: which is to say that, on the lips of most modern indoctrinators, the phrase 'mentally healthy' means much the same as 'conformist'. Yet it is obvious that there are many instances in which a sane man would not conform to society. The notion of defining mental health in quite other terms—in terms, perhaps, of flexibility, freedom, energy, creative ability, and the capacity for enjoyment— would seem dangerous to most modern indoctrinators. For on these criteria we might have to say that someone who enjoyed, say, both heterosexual and homosexual love was as sane, if not saner, than someone whose enjoyment was more narrowly confined: and that would never do. We insist on 'good' people in society in the same way that schoolmasters insist on 'good' boys at school: that is, boys who give no trouble, and shine only in those fields approved of by the educational authorities.

This places a very heavy responsibility on the teaching profession as a whole: the responsibility of insisting that, however irrational adults may be, they have no right to pass on their irrationality to the children. To insist on this means more than to write books or deliver lectures about it. It means using whatever forms of pressure or force are necessary to ensure that teachers are left free not to indoctrinate: to ensure that they are not wholly the instruments of society, but in some sense its leaders. If teachers can strike for more pay, they can also strike for freedom to educate without indoctrinating: for freedom to communicate with children in the spheres of religious and moral belief and behaviour in ways which might not be approved of by parents, local authorities, Ministries, or any other social organ. Unless they do this, it seems to me that they might as well stop being teachers altogether, or resign themselves to the role of social propagandists. At least they must decide whether they are going to serve the Establishment or to serve the truth.

Naturally I do not at all want to say that all teaching in all societies today is indoctrinatory. But I incline to think that most of it is either indoctrinatory or irrelevant to that territory in the human personality which we wish to conquer and which is now occupied by indoctrination. To teach Latin grammar, mathematics, science or modern languages can plainly be useful, but it does not develop and enlarge the personality in the same way as teaching and discussion of those problems and areas of discourse with which people are intimately concerned: discussion of their feelings, their moral behaviour, their religious aspirations, their practical choices. Though society does not object to its children learning things which are irrelevant to this area—things which are either useful to the technological culture, like science, or harmlessly amusing, like classics—it does very strongly object to anyone so much as setting foot without authorization on the area of morality, convention, or however we choose to describe the expressions of the social super-ego.

44

The super-ego does not give ground without a direct conflict. Teach a child basketwork, Arabic grammar, astrology, Tachist painting or musique concrète, and you are all right; the Establishment regards you as harmless, and pseudo-progressives and liberals regard you as advanced. But teach it about sex experimentally, and you get into the national press—almost everyone will join hands in defending the territory that they are *really* concerned with. The direct conflict can only be avoided in marginal issues.

Freud rather despaired of man's ability to regard reality in a scientific spirit, at least in the areas of religion and morality: and it was his determination to do so, rather than any specific principles which he enunciated, that earned him distrust and misinterpretation. It is the notions that we are all irrational and guilt-ridden, that we all turn away from reality, and that only an objective and honest examination of our own personalities and feelings can set this right, which we find frightening. For we are all apt to think that here and now, in twentieth-century England, at least, we are free: we are not subject to the sexual inhibitions of Calvin's régime or the Victorian Age, the political oppression of Hitler or Stalin, the religious intolerance of the Middle Ages and the Inquisition. But of course we are subject to the same oppressions in different forms. Skirts may go up or down, and more or less people may, at least consciously, side with D. H. Lawrence: but sex remains a matter of guilt. Political establishments may vary in tone and function: but in so far as they are imperfect they are necessarily oppressive. And the fact that we may be less religious than our fathers does not give us the right to pat ourselves on the back because we are more tolerant about religion: anybody can be tolerant if he does not care.

In putting before you the concept of indoctrination, and by contrast the concept of education as a counter to indoctrination, I have outlined a task for teachers which involves a great deal of uphill work. It is, necessarily, a slow process, and entails a lot of hard fighting. Some people who tried to do it have been crucified or made to drink hemlock: others have had to live their lives in isolation amid the hostility of society: others again have been forced, because of the immense strength of the opposition, into giving up altogether, and into adopting a conformity which seems easier but which in fact brings death to the soul. The only piece of optimism I can offer is this: that in a world where most men are puppets, pulled hither and thither by the strings of political power or psychological compulsion, only he who deliberately sets his face towards complete freedom can avoid being pulled into the darkness of the mêlée. In the light of modern knowledge, much of what we have learnt to regard as 'great' or 'important' actions, together with the 'great' men in the history books and the men in society today who are commonly believed to have power, seem only, as Matthew Arnold says, to be 'on a darkling plain, Swept with confused alarms of struggle and flight, Where ignorant armies clash by night'. Only those prepared to acknowledge the darkness and look for the light can make any real progress. It is slow, but it is real: and an ounce of reality is worth many tons of fantasy and confusion.

III

ADOLESCENTS INTO ADULTS

by

R. M. HARE

SINCE I am going to criticize Mr. Wilson in some respects, I must start by saying that I am, in all essentials, on the same side as he is. I believe in a distinction between education and indoctrination; and I believe that indoctrination is a bad thing. But I also believe that he stated his case somewhat too extremely; and I think that by so doing he exposed himself to some possible attacks from the propagandists of indoctrination. It is of the highest importance to safeguard Mr. Wilson's liberal views against such attacks; for otherwise advocates of the closed mind and the closed society may find it easier to enlist the support of moderates against Mr. Wilson; and that would be a pity. I want you to realize, therefore, that my criticisms of Mr. Wilson will bulk large in this lecture only because, to avoid repetition, I have left out all those many points on which I should agree with him.

Mr. Wilson thinks that education is a good thing, and indoctrination a bad thing; and it is therefore very important for him to state clearly wherein lies the difference. He considers two possibilities: a distinction on the basis of *method*, and a distinction on the basis of *content*. According to the first distinction, education differs from indoctrination because there is a difference in *how* we teach; according to the second, the difference is a difference in *what* we teach. Mr. Wilson plumps for the second sort of distinction. He rejects a distinction on the basis of method on the following ground. 'Since young children and infants', he says, 'cannot discuss, the methods we use to educate them are bound to resemble hypnosis and brain-washing more than they resemble a democratic exchange of views' (p. 34). So if indoctrination is a kind of method, we shall have to admit that this method has a place in the teaching of young children. But Mr. Wilson does not want to admit this, because he wants to use the word 'indoctrination' for something that is always bad, on whomsoever it is used. So he cannot admit that non-rational methods of teaching, such as we have to use with young children, are indoctrination. So it cannot be the *method* that makes a kind of teaching into indoctrination. So, he thinks, it must be the content—what is taught. We shall avoid indoctrinating our children if we only educate them 'to adopt behaviour-patterns and to have feelings which are seen by every sane and sensible person to be agreeable and necessary. These behaviour-patterns will be rational (he says), in the sense that they derive from reality rather than from the values, fears, desires or prejudices of individual people' (p. 34).

Now this, it seems to me, will not do at all. For who are to count as sane and sensible people? Most people think that they themselves and the majority of their friends are sane and sensible people. So if that is what Mr. Wilson says, he will not succeed in barring the way to a great many educational practices that I am sure he would want to call indoctrination. Take, for example, those Roman Catholics who, as the Archbishop of Liverpool so disarmingly said, 'insist that their children should be entrusted in school to Catholic teachers (because) the teacher's causality'—sinister word—'in the educational process has results in terms of the appreciation of truth, natural and supernatural, standards of values, moral, aesthetic and literary which depend ultimately on the per-

48

sonality of the teacher himself'. These Roman Catholics and the teachers to whom they entrust their children will no doubt all think that they are sane and sensible, and that they are in touch with reality (perhaps they will add, 'natural and supernatural reality'). So when these children have been duly indoctrinated and turned into good Roman Catholics, the parents and teachers will claim not to have offended against Mr. Wilson's canon. And the same can be said if we substitute for 'Roman Catholics', 'Communists', 'Victorians', 'ancient Spartans', 'Trobriand Islanders', or, for that matter, 'Anglicans'. Yet surely Mr. Wilson will want to say, with Dryden, of such a case:

> By education most have been misled;
> So they believe, because they were so bred.
> The priest continues what the nurse began,
> And thus the child imposes on the man.

Dryden, it will be remembered, was speaking of Anglican indoctrination.[1]

If we distinguish indoctrination from education in terms of their content, we are bound to reach this *impasse*. For to make the distinction in this way is to say that there is a *right* content—a *right* doctrine—and, furthermore, that the teacher is the man who knows what it is. It is to say that, provided that this right doctrine is adhered to, it is not indoctrination that is being done, but education. Now I know very well that Mr. Wilson does not want to say this, and that it is inconsistent with other things that he says; but I wanted to show just how easily a clever propagandist could twist his words into something that he and any liberal would abhor.

Now why has Mr. Wilson fallen into this trap of saying that indoctrination is distinguished from education by its content? I think it is because he does not consider a third

---

[1] *The Hind and the Panther*, III, 389.

possibility, besides saying that the distinction is one of content, and saying that it is one of method. This third possibility is that it is one of *purpose*, or *aim*. This series of lectures is about aims in education, so I am surprised that he did not see this third possibility. Perhaps we can discover why he missed it if we consider in more detail what he said about methods. We have to admit, as he does, that in the early stages of the education of young children, some non-rational methods of teaching, especially in matters of moral behaviour, have to be used. But, he seems to argue, if we have to use these methods, it is pointless to condemn them; but we should be condemning them if we called them 'indoctrination'; therefore we must not call them indoctrination. But since the *methods* do not differ fundamentally from some things that we *should* call indoctrination, the difference between indoctrination and other kinds of teaching cannot be one of method. And with all this I want to agree. If you want to keep 'indoctrination' as a bad word, you cannot start using it of methods which everyone thinks legitimate, because inevitable. But it does not follow that the difference is one of content.

Suppose, for example, that one of my children is going through a phase of telling a lot of lies. It may be that its age is such that no rational discussion of the evil consequences of lying is much good; I may engage in such discussion as a kind of lip-service to my liberal principles, but I may know that what will really influence the child to stop lying is not the discussion, but the tone in which it is conducted. Psychologists can perhaps advise on the best method of getting young children out of the habit of lying; but we can be sure that the method will not be, in Mr. Wilson's sense, a rational one. Let us suppose that what happens is that the child senses that I disapprove very strongly of lying, and therefore stops doing it—let us ignore the question of whether this is a psychologically desirable method or not. Have I, by using this non-rational method of affecting the child's behaviour, been *indoctrinating* the child? I do not think so. For I do not *want* the child to remain such that non-rational persuasion or influence is the only kind of moral communication I can have with it. The difference lies in the aim.

There is a German rhyme that I was once taught which goes

> Was der Vater will,
> Was die Mutter spricht,
> Das befolge still.
> Warum? Frage nicht.

> What your father wishes,
> What your mother says,
> Do it in silence.
> Why? Don't ask questions.

Now if I wanted my children to *keep* this sort of attitude to me, or to what I was teaching them, then I should be indoctrinating. But I do not want this. I may have *now* to use non-rational methods of teaching, but my wish is that they may as soon as possible become unnecessary. So, though on occasion I may use the very same methods of teaching as the German who wrote this rhyme, and though my teaching may have exactly the same content, that it is wrong to lie, he is indoctrinating and I am not, because he wants the child always to go on taking its morality from its elders, even after they are dead, whereas I want the child as soon as possible to learn to think morally for itself.

I hope that this example will help you to see what I think is wrong with what some enlightened people say about the moral education of children. One sometimes comes across extreme examples. I know a man who has a child of one year old, and he keeps on saying that he is absolutely determined not to influence his child's moral growth in any way;

the child must find its own morality; to try to influence it would be to 'diminish its human personality' as Mr. Wilson put it (p. 33); and my friend thinks that there is only a difference in degree between such attempts to influence the morality of one's children and the grossest forms of parental violence.

Now this is obviously absurd, and I do not suggest that Mr. Wilson would go as far as this. To begin with, we cannot help influencing our children; the only question is, how, and in what direction. This, I think, Mr. Wilson realizes. And, if we are going to influence them anyway, what can we do but try to influence them in the best direction we can think of? But indoctrination only begins when we are trying to stop the growth in our children of the capacity to think for themselves about moral questions. If all the time that we are influencing them, we are saying to ourselves, 'Perhaps in the end they will decide that the best way to live is quite different from what I'm teaching them; and they will have a perfect right to decide that', then we are not to be accused of indoctrinating. We deserve this name only if we say 'I'll try to make this child such a good Communist, or Roman Catholic, or teach him the American way of life so successfully, that he'll never even be able to ask the question whether, or why, one ought to be these things.'

Now what I have said about the *aim* which distinguishes education from indoctrination has a profound bearing upon both the method and the content of education—only these other things are not fundamental; they come from the aim, not it from them. If you are wanting your child in the end to become an adult and think for himself about moral questions, you will try, all the time that you are influencing him by non-rational methods (as you have to), to interest him in rational thinking about morality (this, I know, is a rather solemn expression, but I will try to explain what I mean by it later). That is why I said that I might talk to my child about the evil consequences of lying even though I knew that that was not what would really stop him lying. You can tell what are the aims of a teacher, and whether they are indoctrinatory or not, by studying his methods. Suppose that he carefully arranges for there not to be any free and open discussion of questions of morality until he is absolutely certain that his pupils have, by non-rational methods, been got into a state where they are bound all to give the 'right' answers. Or suppose that he takes enormous care that, though his pupils are encouraged to read books, the books are all ones which say the same thing. Then we shall know what his object is; it is to prevent them asking the questions that might cause them in the end to come to a different moral attitude from himself. Suppose that, on the other hand, he really senses that his pupils are perplexed about some moral question—about sex, for example, or pacifism—and, seeing this, is prepared to discuss it with them, with no holds barred and no questions banned, and is himself prepared to ask the questions again—really ask them—and is prepared to answer them in a different way from the way he has up till now, if that is the way the argument goes. Then we know that he is concerned to get his pupils to think for themselves.

This matter of the teacher himself really treating the questions as open ones is crucial. There is no possibility of pretence here; one cannot act this sort of thing, though we all know parsons and schoolmasters who try. Mr. Wilson said something that may mislead when he said that 'questions of moral integrity, honesty, or overt truthfulness do not arise. We live in a mad world; what counts is not preserving our own integrity, but making the world saner' (p. 41). I understood what he meant; he meant that we all sometimes have to temporize with the powers that be. But in our dealings with the young, nothing short of absolute integrity will do.

Yet it is not easy really to give one's own deepest moral opinions a turning over. This, however, is what we have to do if we are going to have honest discussions with younger people about the moral problems that perplex them. Because it is a painful process, various ways have been devised of making it less painful. But they are only pretences.

There is the expedient of discussing questions which do not really hurt—academic questions which might have troubled people once but are not the ones that worry us now. There is the even worse expedient of taking questions that really do worry us, but discussing them in a superficial debating style without really becoming involved in them. This is a thing that the young will often do when they have not yet got personally involved in some moral question. It is a thing that they should *never* be encouraged to do, about serious questions.

If a teacher is willing to engage in serious and honest discussion with his pupils about moral questions, to the extent that they are able, then he is not an indoctrinator, even though he may also, because of their age, be using non-rational methods of persuasion. These methods are not, as is commonly supposed, bad in themselves; they are bad only if they are used to produce attitudes that are not open to argument. The fact that a teacher does not himself have such attitudes is the guarantee that he is not an indoctrinator.

I said that the difference in aim between education and indoctrination will result in a difference in content. This is because of the methods which, as we have seen, are appropriate to these two aims. The method appropriate to indoctrination shelters both teacher and pupil from the fresh winds of argument, and this is bound to have the result that things will get taught which would not get taught if the whole process were exposed to these breezes. If the teacher speaks with the voice of authority, however cunningly disguised, and is prepared to use every persuasive device to close the minds of his pupils, there is almost no limit to the irrational taboos and myths that he can successfully inculcate. If, on the other hand, the pupils are not protected against other influences, and the only pressure on them is to consider seriously and rationally what is said and come to their own decisions about it, then it will be less possible to put over these received opinions, and what can be put over will to a certain extent have its content circumscribed. Irrational attitudes cannot flourish when rational methods of argument are seriously practised.

I must say a word here about the attitude a teacher ought to take to the various outside influences, most of them non-rational, which all the time surround his pupils in the press, television, etc. Mr. MacIntyre has said something about these; and I do not dissent from the value-judgments he made about the need for encouraging a critical spirit. But why did he have to be so *gloomy*? Knowing him, I was sorry to see him assuming—I hope only temporarily—the mantle of the professional literary pessimist. I was even sorrier to see Mr. Wilson, briefly, joining in this familiar chorus; for I myself am much more inclined to sympathize with the attitude of Professor Medawar when he said recently,

The Predicament of Man is all the rage now that people have sufficient leisure and are sufficiently well fed to contemplate it, and many a tidy little literary reputation has been built on exploiting it; anybody nowadays who dared to suggest that the plight of man might not be wholly desperate would get a sharp rap over the knuckles in any literary weekly (*Mind*, 1961, p. 105).

The state of the world is bad enough in all conscience with-out adding a dose of quite factitious depression. We might even get so engrossed in moaning about the mess we are in that we became unable to do any constructive thinking about how to improve matters. Indeed, if we do not look out, then Mr. MacIntyre will label us 'improvers' (happy term!) if we so much as suggest that there *is* any way in which the world could be made better.

But I hope that teachers, when they rightly take Mr. MacIntyre's advice and teach their pupils to criticize what they see around them, will make it clear that 'criticize' is being used in the sense of 'appraise' and not of 'find fault with'. Otherwise they will only be producing a brood of grumblers who have closed their minds to hope. Rather, I would say, teach them to look up out of their books sometimes—even if the books are novels by the most favoured authors; teach them to look out of the window; teach them sometimes, even, to go out of the door—and *look*. If the view that they see is good, or has good in it (as it always will have if they look), teach them to enjoy it, and to help others to enjoy it. If it is bad, or has something bad in it (as it always will), teach them to *think*: What can I do to make it better? How can I get other people to help me make it better—even if people like Mr. MacIntyre call us 'improvers' for our pains. This, surely, is better than breaking out into barren and futile jeremiads. But I must not digress.

I was talking about the influences of the press and television. Surely the harm that these do has been somewhat exaggerated, and the good correspondingly underrated. Take advertisements, for example. If all the advertisements were advertising the same brand of soap, as might be the case in a Communist country, then it would be time to get worried—though even in that case good would come of encouraging people to wash. But since they are all advertising different brands, the consumer very soon realizes that there is not much difference between the brands, and, though of course he will probably go on buying *some* heavily advertised brand, will not very much care which. The same applies to more important things than soap. Advertisements keep branded goods before our attention; and if this is not done, we shall probably stop buying them and buy some other brand. But in choosing between the brands which are competing in this way, does not the multiplicity of the advertisements make us stop caring which we buy, unless, indeed, we think there is a real difference between the brands. If we do, and if we think it is important to have the best one, do we not then make some effort to find out which the best one is? This, at any rate, is what the schools ought to be teaching their pupils to do; and I do not think it is so difficult. Listen to any two young men discussing the merits of two kinds of motor-car. Which influences them the most—the blurbs in the advertisements or the reports of performance in the technical press, which they read avidly? I must admit that they are also influenced by the appearance of the cars; but ought they not to be? Are we not continually told by the supporters of good industrial design, of whom I am one, to *look* at what we are buying?[1]

The same applies, with very few changes, to politics, morals and religion. If there is plenty of variety in the market

[1] This lecture was delivered some time before the appearance of the Pilkington Report. I do not wish these remarks to be taken as supporting the opponents of the report. The danger of commercial television is not that it provides a large quantity of popular entertainment—any medium which serves a mass audience is bound to do this. The danger is rather that if commercial advantage only is followed, this kind of programme will push out everything else, or almost so. What is needed in broadcasting and television is not to reduce the quantity of low-brow programmes but to improve their quality, and at the same time to provide an ample and varied supply of programmes for educated people. If this is done, and if schoolmasters do their job, I am optimistic enough to predict that an ever-growing audience will listen to or watch them. But I think that this is more likely to happen if the public-service side of television is strengthened in the way the Report recommends.

place, discernment and discrimination will be fostered. That is one reason why I have the deepest misgivings about what is euphemistically called 'Church Unity'. It is true that all Christians ought to be able to worship at the same table, and to live and pray together without acrimony. And I am convinced that nothing now prevents them doing this but the purely political rivalries between the various ecclesiastical machines. But in order to bring about unity of worship, is it necessary to have a single 'church' in the organizational sense? It seems to me that to do this would be to create a religious monopoly of the most pernicious kind, a sort of totalitarian church, whose main function would be to perpetuate the power of its leaders to indoctrinate and thereby control. So I hope that you will not misunderstand me when I say that more good than harm comes from competition, both in commerce and in politics and in religion.

So, by and large, I think that schoolmasters have little to fear from the press and television, provided that there is diversity, and provided that the schoolmasters are themselves trying to educate and not to indoctrinate. Nor, I should like to add, subject to the same proviso, have they anything to fear from philosophers. You may have noticed, as I did, a rather sinister letter which appeared in *The Times* recently. A correspondent, writing about a project to build a Roman Catholic hostel in Oxford, which had been condemned by the Roman Catholic chaplaincy as a breach of a gentlemen's agreement to abstain from proselytizing, complained that the really bad proselytizing in Oxford was done on behalf of atheists by some people he called 'analytical philosophers', who had, he said, destroyed the faith of three young Anglican friends of his. He seemed unaware that the group of philosophers whom he calls 'analytical' contains several devout Roman Catholics, as well as some devout Anglicans. What had happened to his friends was, I am sure, something like this: before they came to Oxford, they had been indoctrinated by their parents or schoolmasters with some spurious arguments for religion; when they got to the university and came to see that the arguments were bogus, they reacted, perhaps temporarily, in the opposite direction. But this is the fault of people who think that they are doing a service to religion by this kind of indoctrination. I never do anything of this kind, but practise 'analytical philosophy' according to my ability; yet about one of my pupils in every twelve has become a parson.

There was one more gap in Mr. Wilson's exposition that I should like to fill, if I can. Having distinguished between education and indoctrination in terms of their contents, it was important for him to state clearly the distinction between the contents of these two things. This he did not do, though he gave examples; and I have already said that it is no use saying that we can avoid indoctrination if we teach only those moral opinions that sane and sensible people would agree with—for who are the sane and sensible people? Now I have maintained, for this very reason, that a distinction in terms of content will not do; but that if we have the aim of educating people, this aim will determine the method, and the method will to a certain extent determine the content. But this is not nearly specific enough; I am sure that you will want to ask me what, in more detail, *is* this method of rational discussion that I have been advocating, and why I think that it will be inimical to what I have called myths and taboos and will let in only rational opinions.

Now to ask this is to ask me to launch out into a treatise on moral philosophy. I could not possibly say anything at all profound in the time remaining.[1] But I will try to give you an outline of what I think. The two essential features of

[1] I have said what I can on this subject in a recent book, *Freedom and Reason*, Oxford, 1963.

moral opinions are, first, that they are not about matters of fact but about how one ought to behave (this is what is meant by calling moral judgments 'prescriptive'); and secondly, that if I hold a certain moral opinion about an act done by one person, I must hold the same moral opinion about a similar act done by a similar person in similar circumstances. This is often referred to by moral philosophers as the principle of the 'universalizability' of moral judgments. Both of these are *logical* features of moral judgments; if we do not understand either of them, we do not understand the uses of the moral words. Roughly speaking, a moral opinion is *rational* if it is not taken on authority as a matter of fact but freely accepted as a prescription for living, and if it is recognized as holding good irrespective of whether it is I that am the subject of it or someone else. The reason why, if someone transgresses either of these two requirements, he is not being rational, is that they are requirements of logic, having their basis in the meanings of the moral words; therefore someone who transgresses them is being as illogical as someone who says 'All the books are red but there is one which is not.'

Now the consequences of the first of these features of moral judgments for moral discussion have been adequately dealt with by Mr. Wilson. Briefly, since moral judgments are not statements of fact or pieces of information, they cannot be taught out of a text-book like the names of the capitals of European countries. It is not a question of *informing* those whom we are teaching, but of their coming to accept a certain opinion for their own.

But Mr. Wilson did not, so far as I can remember, say anything about the second feature. Now, as I could show if I had time, it is this feature, in conjunction with the first, which really limits the moral opinions that we can hold. It is by applying these two characteristics of moral judgments together that argument really gets a grip on moral questions. What we have to teach people, if we are educating them morally, is to ask themselves the question 'What kind of behaviour am I ready to prescribe for myself, given that in prescribing it for myself, I am prescribing it also for anybody in a like situation?' I could, but I will not, go on to show how this question, if we can get people to ask it, circumscribes their moral choices in a rational way, so that the abandonment of taboos and irrational prejudices which Mr. Wilson recommends does not, as has sometimes been feared, open the way to unbridled license.

I said, 'If we can get people to ask it.' But one of the most important things for educators to remember is that morality, as governed by this question, is a very *difficult* thing to accept. Because it is a difficult and sophisticated thing, it does not come naturally to children. It is no use, as Mr. Wilson sometimes seems to imply, merely leaving children as free as possible from external moral influences, and hoping that the thing will just grow. It *will* grow in most cases, but only because the seed is there in our own way of thinking, from which it is well-nigh impossible to isolate a child. It is not, however, something innate; it is a question of tradition; morality is something that has to be handed down; if it were not—if the process were interrupted—our children really would grow up as barbarians.

What has to be passed on is not any *specific* moral principle, but an understanding of what morality is and a readiness to think in a moral way and act accordingly. This could be put in other words by saying that children have to learn to use the moral words such as 'right' and 'wrong' and to understand their meaning. That is why it is so very important for philosophers to study what their meaning is—how silly it is to say that philosophers ought not to occupy themselves with matters of words! It must be emphasized that it is not the content of any particular morality that is being handed down—that would be indoctrination, if the aim was, at all costs, to implant *these* particular moral principles. It is not a particular morality, but morality itself that we are teaching; not to think this or that (because we say so or because the good and great have said so) but to think morally for oneself. And to learn this is to learn how to *speak* morally, understanding what one says.

Doubtless it is not possible in practice to pass on the mere form of morality without embodying it in some content; we cannot teach children the abstract idea of a moral principle as such without teaching them some concrete moral principles. And naturally we shall choose for this purpose those principles which we think in themselves desirable. This, as I said, is not indoctrination provided that our aim is that the children should in the end come to appraise these principles for themselves. Just so, one cannot teach the scientific outlook without teaching some science; but the science that is taught could be radically altered in the light of later researches, and yet the scientific outlook remain. The good science teacher will teach what he thinks to be the truth, but his teaching will not have proved vain if what has been taught is later rejected as false; and similarly, if we can teach children what morality is, using our own moral thinking as an example, we shall have done our job, even if the moral thinking which they later do leads them to different conclusions.

Fortunately there is a close connexion between the form of morality and its content. As I could show if there were time, and have attempted to show in my book which I have already referred to, once the form of morality is accepted in our thinking, it quite narrowly circumscribes the substance of the moral principles that we shall adopt. We can therefore happily start by securing the adherence of our children—if necessary by non-rational methods—to the moral principles which we think best, provided that these are consistent with the form of morality; but we must leave them at liberty later to think out for themselves different principles, subject to the same proviso.

Now in conveying to children what morality is, our method is governed by what it is that we are trying to convey. Because moral judgments are things that one has to make for oneself, we have to get children to understand, in the end, that 'wrong' does *not* mean 'what the parent or the schoolmaster forbids'; the schoolmaster might forbid it, and the child might still think it right, and the child might have a right to its opinion. On this aspect of the matter Mr. Wilson has laid enough stress.

But secondly, and arising out of the universalizability of moral judgments, the child has got to realize, somehow, that what is wrong for another to do to him is wrong for him to do to another. This is the foundation of all that part of morality which concerns our dealings with other people. And this gives us an important clue about method. Children must learn to think about what it is like to be the other person. They must cultivate their sympathetic imaginations. And this is not easy. It will not be brought about without effort on the part of parents and schoolmasters. And it will not be brought about by rational discussion alone. Suppose that somebody who took Mr. Wilson too literally, and did not realize the importance of this feature of morality which he left out, went away from his lecture determined to confine himself, in his dealings with the young, in the early stages to plain imperatives like 'Go to bed', which make no pretence to be moral and therefore can do no harm, and in the later stages to rational discussion. His charges really would, if he could observe this principle in isolation from other influences, grow up without an understanding of morality.

63

Of course, this is unlikely to happen in practice, because there are, fortunately, other influences on children than their parents and schoolmasters, and many of them are media for the handing on of an understanding of moral thinking. The mere use of moral words by a child's contemporaries does a great deal. So nobody is going to be able to carry out this too literal interpretation of Mr. Wilson's prescription; and we are in no real danger of relapsing into a Hobbesian state of nature, in which every man's hand is against every man. But unless *some* non-rational methods are used, it is unlikely that all our children will come to absorb this principle as deeply as we could wish; and to that extent less of their thinking about action will be moral thinking, and their actions will show this.

The non-rational influences I have in mind are chiefly two; environment, and example. The examples that one has set before one are *part* of one's environment, so this division is not a neat one; but it will do for what I want to say. The first important thing, if we want our children to learn morality, is that they should be put into an environment in which the unpleasant effects of other people's lapses on them are as obvious as possible. This means that they must have plenty of opportunity of rubbing up against other people in some sort of more or less constant group—more or less constant, because they have to have time to get to think of the other people in the group as people (i.e. as like themselves), or the treatment will not work. In such an environment, children can easily absorb the lesson that they ought to do unto others as they would that others should do unto them. The family is such a group; but families are not enough, because some families fall down on the job, and delinquency is sometimes the result. Schools, therefore, have a lot to contribute, as have clubs; and they have one very important advantage over the family, that in them the child rubs up against a large number of people of his own age, whom, therefore, it is easy for him to think of as like himself, sharing his likes and dislikes, and therefore hurt by the things that hurt him and pleased by the things that please him. It will be easier in such a group for the child to learn to universalize his moral judgments.

Secondly, the group must have a good tradition. If it is a St. Trinian's, the child will indeed suffer from the misdeeds of other children, but its reaction will be one of self-defence merely, and we shall have a reign of blackboard jungle law. There has to be a tradition of kindness to, and co-operation with, other people. I am sorry to repeat these platitudes; but I want to show you how they are the consequences of the nature of morality; *that* they are true is obvious, but we need to understand *why* they are true.

But, thirdly, how do we start these good traditions? This seems to me to be the most important, perhaps the only essential, function of the adult in moral education. After a certain age, children and young people will get their moral ideas and ideals and attitudes for the most part from each other; either from their schoolfellows or from the rest of the gang. So the most important point at which the adult can intervene, *if* he can intervene, is by influencing the morality of the group; and this is done by example.

Now I do not want you to make at this point what I think is a very easy mistake to make. 'Setting a good example' by itself is no use at all. The people to whom it is being set must want to follow it. We need to know what can make them want to follow it. I think that all good schoolmasters know the answer to this question. Children desire to imitate particular traits of a person whom they desire to imitate as a whole. If an adult is *merely* an example of desirable moral attitudes, they will not take much notice. But if there are a great many other things about him that they admire—usually things that have nothing to do with morals—then they will swallow the moral attitudes too.

There are a lot of things that children and young men will willingly learn from their elders. Sometimes, if they are intellectually gifted, they will even willingly learn from them Latin and French; but this is unfortunately not common. They will, however, very frequently be anxious to learn to play football, or sail boats, or play the violin in the orchestra; and if there is an adult whom they trust to teach them these things, they will pick up from him much besides. That is why those who are employing schoolmasters look, not merely for good teachers of Latin or French or football or music—they look for men who, in teaching these things, will hand on something that is of much more importance.

This is one of the sources of the value of so-called out-of-school activities like games and music, as well as the more wide-ranging ones like sailing and mountaineering, which are now becoming so popular. They are vehicles for the transmission of an understanding of morality from one generation to another. But they also have another importance from the moral point of view: all of them, to a greater or less extent, are co-operative activities; they therefore require, in all who participate in them, a standard of behaviour. On a small scale, but intensely, they reproduce those very factors which, I suppose, have led to the development of morality in civilized communities at large. One learns, in such teams or groups, to submit oneself to a rule—a rule not dictated by some particular person, but freely accepted by all the participants, either because, like the rule about not passing forward, or like watching the conductor, it is a necessary condition for the doing of *this* particular activity called orchestral playing or rugger; or else because it is dictated by the realities of the situation, like not sailing by the lee, or not getting lost in the mountains and causing other people to organize search parties to rescue you. The second of these two kinds of rules are the more important; and therefore I think that the second of the two kinds of activity —that which includes sailing and fell walking—deserves the increasing attention that it is getting from schoolmasters. Perhaps music should be after all included with these; for music also is in touch with reality; if you play a wrong note it is not just that you have broken the rule of a game. But games, in the narrow sense, will always have a certain artificiality. And of course compulsory games, whose rules are not freely accepted by the participants, do no good at all from the point of view that we are considering, though they may have some of the other virtues that used to be claimed for them.

The point that I wish to emphasize by saying these familiar things is that these practices, which schoolmasters have found useful, owe their usefulness to the nature of what they are trying to hand on, namely morality. Morality has, of its nature, to be freely accepted; therefore in this respect the rules of seamanship are a better analogue of it—and their strict observance actually a better example of it—than the rules in the school rule-book. And secondly, morality is impartial as between persons; therefore, to learn to accept rules applicable impartially within a group is a good schooling in morality. There is, of course, a danger in this; we all know the kind of team spirit which counts anything as fair against the other side, or against those outside the team. To become a loyal member of a group is an important step on the way from egoism to altruism; but it is a step at which it is all too easy to get stuck.

I must add here that, important as membership of groups is in the formation of moral ideas, it is important also for the development of the individual's personality that he should be able sometimes to break away from the group and pursue his own ideals, if necessary entirely by himself, if he is that sort of person. For all morality is not social morality—to think that it is, is a mistake that has often been made by moral philosophers and by educationists. There are moral ideals, some of them very fine ones, which have nothing to do with our fellow men; and although it is necessary to learn to live with our fellow men, it is restricting to the personality to be unable to get away from them. This educational requirement has, like the others, a theoretical basis in moral philosophy; but for reasons of time I shall not be able to tell you what it is.

I have mentioned two ways in which adults can help to pass on the idea of morality to another generation. But the power of adults to do this is severely limited by what adolescents will accept from adults. They want to imitate adults; but they want to imitate them in one thing above all —*in being adult*. They want, that is to say, to be their own masters. They will only feel that they have really succeeded in imitating the adult when they have got the adult out of the way.

This lends peculiar interest to an experiment which you may have seen described in *The Times* recently.[1] At Crawley, the local authority, having available some Nissen huts in a clearing in some woods near the town, turned them over without supervision to various youth organizations to use for a variety of purposes ranging from, I think, boxing to making model aeroplanes. The huts were intensively used, and looked after with very little damage, and obviously filled a need which must exist in other places than Crawley. When I say 'without supervision', this is not strictly accurate; there is a forest warden of the Forestry Commission who lives on the spot and keeps a fatherly eye on the buildings. But the point is that all the organization is done by the

[1] *The Times*, Feb. 18, 1961, p. 9.

groups themselves without any adult interference. The success of this experiment should not make us ask, as apparently some people have asked, 'Are youth leaders (or for that matter schoolmasters) really necessary?' For of course good youth leaders and good schoolmasters will always be in short supply; what we learn from this experiment is one way of making the supply go further. Sometimes the best way adults can help adolescents to grow up is by keeping in the background; and of course this lesson has an application in schools too, and still more in universities.

It is by this readiness to retire gracefully, indeed, that we can most easily tell the educator from the indoctrinator. I said earlier that I agreed with Mr. Wilson that education might sometimes have to use the same methods as indoctrination, and that therefore the two cannot be distinguished by their methods. I said that they were distinguished by their aims; the educator is trying to turn children into adults; the indoctrinator is trying to make them into perpetual children. But I said that the aim would all the same make a difference to the method; and this becomes evident, if we watch the process over a period. Many of the methods I have alluded to can be used for indoctrination in the most deplorable doctrines; the Nazi youth organizations used them, fortunately without lasting success, to pervert a whole generation of German youth while they thought they were just youth-hostelling or playing games or whatever it might be. But if one watches carefully one will notice a difference. The educator is waiting and hoping all the time for those whom he is educating to start *thinking*; and none of the thoughts that may occur to them are labelled 'dangerous' *a priori*. The indoctrinator, on the other hand, is watching for signs of trouble, and ready to intervene to suppress it when it appears, however oblique and smooth his methods may be. The difference between these two is like the difference between the colonial administrator who knows, and is pleased, that he is working himself out of a job, and the one who is determined that the job shall still be there even when he himself retires.

So there is, in the end, a very great difference between the two methods. At the end of it all, the educator will insensibly stop being an educator, and find that he is talking to an equal, to an educated man like himself—a man who may disagree with everything he has ever said; and, unlike the indoctrinator, he will be pleased. So, when this happens, you can tell from the expression on his face which he is.

IV

'MENTAL HEALTH'
AS AN EDUCATIONAL AIM[1]

by

R. S. PETERS

Introduction

IN England we are developing a highly differentiated society and we are often warned that we shall soon have not merely two nations but a league of nations without a common culture and shared ideals. This should not surprise us; for where are such unifying ideals to be fostered? The study of literature, history and the classics has had to be cut down to make room for the vast expansion in scientific education without which our society cannot survive, and the Church is rapidly losing the authority it once had as the source of unifying ideals. We tend to treat the doctor who looks after our bodies and the psychiatrist who looks after our minds with more respect than we treat the priest who advises us about our souls—if we still think we have one. For they are scientists; and it is scientists who are now coming to be thought of as repositories of wisdom about the mysteries of life.

This general trend explains why the educationist sometimes

[1] This article, which is based on a talk given on the B.B.C. Third Programme, was read as a paper to the Philosophy of Education Society at Harvard in March 1961. The author wishes to express his thanks to those participants in the discussion whose comments led to minor alterations and additions to the paper. It was first presented in embryonic form at the Department of Education in Manchester in 1960.

inclines his ear towards a new expert, the psychologist, when he is at loss to find new unifying educational ideals to replace the old religious ones. There is thus much talk in educational circles of 'the mental health of the child', 'wholeness', 'integration', 'adjustment', and all that sort of thing[1]. We no longer talk of turning out Christian gentlemen; we talk of letting people develop mental health or mature personalities. In America, so we are told, Freud's priestly role is much more explicitly acknowledged. Philip Rieff, for instance, in his recent book called Freud, *the Mind of the Moralist*,[2] sees Freud as the prophet of 'psychological man', the final product of the quarrel of Western man with his own spirit. The classical legacy of political man, he declares, is an archaism; the Christian legacy of religious man has been repudiated; and experience has revealed the emptiness of the optimistic liberal picture of economic man. Freud heralded the advent of psychological man, the egoist trained in cautious prudence.

This estimation of Freud's role as a moralist may bear witness to the great influence of Freud on American intellectuals; to an Englishman it sounds somewhat quaint—rather like regarding Marx as the prophet of the health services. Nevertheless the general trend is with us, as is shown in the frequent references to psychological notions such as 'mental health' in discussion about educational ideals.

The Concept of 'Human Nature'

What, then, is the nature of such ideals and how far can the psychologist take us in justifying them? It might first of all be pointed out, of course, that 'mental health' as an ideal is

[1] See, for instance, W. Allinsmith and G. Goethals, *The Role of the School in Mental Health*, Basic Books, New York, 1960.

[2] I. P. Rieff, *Freud, the Mind of the Moralist*, Viking Press, New York, 1955.

obviously a normative notion and that moral philosophers have demonstrated conclusively the illegitimacy of passing from facts about man's nature to normative ideals. This is obvious and banal; the more interesting question is *how far* psychological considerations can take us in establishing such ideals. The psychologist would, presumably, have to start from generalizations about human nature. But his initial difficulty is to give much in the way of content to the concept of a general human nature. There is an obvious and important sense, of course, in which he must, like Aristotle, assume such a general human nature. Men, he could say, have wants, but reason about them; they deliberate and choose and impose rules on them; they adopt plans and schedules. They are not just drawn towards goals like moths towards a light.

Now such a formal account is, as a matter of fact, very important if we are concerned with bringing out what is distinctively human; and, as will be seen later, it is indispensable to the notion of 'mental health'. Nevertheless, from the point of view of an empirical psychologist it is deficient because it lacks content; it merely articulates the sort of concepts that are necessary for describing typically human actions and activities.

The content of the scheme is filled in by reference to the standards of particular societies. That which a man wants, that for the sake of which he acts, his end, is something that has been picked out and named as a result of a particular social life which has reached the level of describing, explaining, and justifying what a man does. Dogs can only be said to wait for their dinner by analogy with men; for it is the framework of rules and standards that converts a substance into 'food' and which makes it part of our 'dinner'; and it is by reference to ends like 'eating dinner', 'getting married', and 'getting promotion' that we give content to our explanatory schemes. What we call 'human nature' will

73

therefore vary from society to society; and there is not much future in trying to erect any universal standards of what is good for man on that basis, unless we have in mind an ideal such as 'adjustment'. But a man could be perfectly 'adjusted' if he conformed to the standards of a Nazi society; and few psychologists would want to hold up the Nazi mentality as an ideal of mental health or of the good for man.

But must accounts of human nature to which a psychologist would appeal in justifying an ideal such as that of 'mental health' be as culture-bound as this? Is there nothing in terms of the contents of human nature which could provide counsels which escape the local autonomy of differing cultural standards? Could not, for instance, the followers of Freud make a case for wants which are varied in their manifestations but universal in their insistence—like those for food, sex, and safety? Any man ignores these at his peril in spite of the fact that what counts as appropriate objects for such wants will vary from culture to culture.

Basic Needs and Mental Health

When we come to a level like this, which is the level of basic needs, we have indeed come to a point where the psychologist may be able to give advice which is not altogether culture-bound; but it is important to be clear about the sort of advice it is and how essentially limited it is. For the notion of 'needs', to which the doctrine appeals, really presupposes the notion of 'wants'. What a man needs is that which it would be injurious for him not to have. But the standard of what constitutes injury depends on what a man wants. We speak of a man's need for money. But what is money necessary for? Presumably for things like his dinner which is something that he wants. And if we say that any man needs food, that is because it is necessary for keeping alive which, presumably, everyone wants to do. But to be alive, unless we are merely talking about keeping our hearts beating, involves the satisfaction of a variety of wants. Thus, although the manner of being alive, the wants that are thought to be worth satisfying, will vary according to personal and cultural preferences, there are, it could be argued, at least some things, like food, water and oxygen, which are necessary conditions for the satisfaction of any other wants, whatever these wants may be.

The psychologist, however, speaks of love and safety as needs, not just of water, food and oxygen. What are these more intangible things necessary for? The answer is that the psychologists have shown them to be necessary for the realistic development and effective *regulation* of wants within a system, whatever the system may be. The miser, for instance, has a style of life which is witness to the need for safety being satisfied in a way which disregards the need for love and to love. A man may come to see money not as what it is—a means of satisfying other wants—but as something valuable in itself. And this irrational want may spread like a cancer until a man's whole outlook becomes distorted and warped. Similarly a paranoid's estimation of every situation is constantly distorted by the all-intrusive thought that people are plotting against him.

And so we return, after a detour, to the rather formal notion of what is essentially human from which we started —the rationality of man as exhibited in his realistic appraisal of himself and his environment and in the regulation of his wants. And, in spite of its formal character, this conception of man as essentially rational not only provides a standard for psychological counsel which is not culture-bound but also includes most of the conceptions of 'mental health' which are current in the literature on the subject. To establish this latter point I propose to consider the six approaches to a concept of 'mental health' which Marie Jahoda distinguishes in her acute and commendably short work on the subject.[1]

Jahoda's Six Criteria of 'Mental Health'

Jahoda, after an exhaustive examination of different psychological conceptions of 'mental health', thinks that they all fall under one or more of the following six criteria:

(i) Self-awareness and self-acceptance.
(ii) Growth and self-actualization.
(iii) Integration.
(iv) Autonomy.
(v) Perception of reality.
(vi) Environmental mastery.

I wish to show that all these notions except one can either be subsumed under the more general notion of 'rationality' or be shown to be one of the 'needs' already distinguished whose satisfaction is a necessary condition of such rationality.

Of the above six criteria Jahoda herself explicitly links the last three with the individual's relation to reality. Her fifth criterion of 'perception of reality' is the clearest case of this. This may be manifest, first of all, in perception that is free from need-distortion, which is the reverse of that of the psychotic. Situations, of course, can be appraised in terms of a variety of objective criteria on the basis of which what is really so can be distinguished from how it may appear to a particular percipient. To be rational implies, amongst other things, to be disposed to assess situations in terms of such objective criteria; to be irrational is to see them under the aspect of what is needed or wished for. A 'mentally healthy' or rational person, on this view, will seek evidence to dis-

[1] M. Jahoda, *Current Concepts of Positive Mental Health*, Basic Books, New York, 1958.

tinguish between what he wishes a situation to be and what it really is, even if his finding goes against his wishes. 'One lacking in mental health will not seek evidence, or will reject it, if it is presented to him and does not suit him' (p. 52). This freedom from distortion is also sometimes stressed in the context of knowledge of others, where additional sensitivity is required in order to perceive situations from the other person's standpoint and thus to anticipate and predict his behaviour. This is surely a capacity for objectivity in a context where such objectivity is notoriously difficult.

The sixth criterion of 'environmental mastery' includes a rather ill-assorted rag-bag. The ability to love, for instance, is often stressed; but on my view this features as a basic need, as a necessary condition for rational behaviour and hence for 'mental health' as well as an exemplification of it, where 'love' may refer either to a capacity for affection or to the more specialized neo-Freudian notion of 'genitality' as the 'potential capacity to develop orgastic potency in relation to a loved partner of the opposite sex' (p. 55). Similarly 'adequacy in personal relationship', which is another quality falling under this criterion, is a combination of realistic appraisal of others and of not being stunted by an inability to care for them. Others stress adequacy in work and play or a more general ability to master the environment, or to adapt efficiently to it, which is exemplified in the carrying out of tasks and roles. Such notions surely fall under the general requirement of practical rationality, the effective imposition of plans and rules on wants. Jahoda makes this explicit in her own requirement for mental health in which emphasis is laid on efficiency in problem-solving behaviour (pp. 62–4). There may well also be some basic need for mastery or achievement underlying such behaviour which is on the same psychological level as the need for love and security already dealt with in my account of basic needs.

White's notion of 'competence' would cover the sort of thing which I have in mind.[1]

'Autonomy', Jahoda's fourth criterion of mental health, is clearly related to rationality in that there is a long-standing tradition which equates rationality with self-determination in the sense of acting on thought-out principles. Thus Jahoda's last three criteria are clearly related to the concept of reality in so far as this includes the capacity for forming rational beliefs, for taking efficient and socially appropriate means to ends, and for acting on thought-out principles.

There is, however, another notion often associated with rationality which is that of *regulation* of wants in relation to each other by foreseeing the consequences of satisfying them and imposing schedules on them in terms of practicality, compatibility and compossibility, so that the individual is not involved in perpetual frustrations and conflicts. And this notion takes care of Jahoda's third criterion, which is the much vaunted 'integration of the personality'—a notion as old as the Greek one of the harmony of the soul. This 'balance of psychic forces in the individual' (pp. 36–9) implies, in Freudian terms, the accommodation by the Ego of the Id and Super-ego without eliminating or denying their demands. This is made possible, in part, on the view of psychologists such as Allport, by the adoption of some 'world-view' which unifies an individual's outlook, especially by the singling out of long-range goals. It would indeed be impossible to impose such schedules on wants and to make decisions about priorities without general rules and the distinction between long-term and short-term interests. Whether much more than this is involved in a 'world-view' is difficult to say. The notion of a 'world-view', like that of 'commitment', has emotional overtones to it which

[1] R. White, 'Competence and the Psycho-sexual Stages of Development' in *Nebraska Symposium on Motivation*, 1960.

convey different things to different people. Certainly little more than a basis on which decisions about priorities can be made is required for 'integration'. Those who are able to regulate their wants in this way are often spoken of as having 'frustration tolerance' or as being able to 'delay gratification'. Tension does not put them into a panic (p. 42).

Jahoda's first criterion of realistic awareness and acceptance of oneself is easy enough, too, to include in the unifying notion of the rationality of man. For ever since Socrates those who have believed in developing man's rationality have stressed the importance of self-knowledge and self-acceptance. Allport stresses what he calls

self-objectification, that peculiar detachment of the mature person when he surveys his own pretensions in relation to his abilities, his present objectives in relation to possible objectives for himself, his own equipment in comparison with the equipment of others, and his opinion of himself in relation to the opinion others hold of him (p. 26).

This does not imply undue preoccupation with oneself, but a realistic estimate of oneself when such an estimate is appropriate. This, of course, is a particular case of the criterion of realistic belief. Fromm makes this explicit when he describes mental health as characterized by 'the grasp of reality inside and outside of ourselves, that is, by the development of objectivity and reason' (p. 27).

I come now to the only one of Jahoda's criteria which it is difficult to incorporate in this analysis—the second one of growth or self-actualization. And there is a good reason for this; for, in my view, it goes beyond both a limited notion of rationality and beyond that of 'mental health'. And that, as I shall hope to show, is why it is the special concern of the educator rather than that of the psychiatrist. It will be worthwhile, therefore, to consider this second criterion more carefully.

Self-actualization and Civilization

To date, the analysis of 'mental health' has dealt only with the development and regulation of wants in a manner which is realistic, undistorted, and comparatively free from conflict. Nothing has been said about which wants are worth satisfying. What has been stressed, however, is that a man can develop undistorted wants and regulate his wants effectively only if his basic needs are not grossly thwarted. This effective regulation of a system of wants is often referred to as 'the integration of personality' or 'mental health'. The psychologist has laid bare some of the conditions which militate against its development. He is thus in a position to prescribe certain things which men need above the level of food, water and oxygen. For unless we satisfy our needs for love and safety we shall be for ever at sixes and sevens with ourselves, not satisfying a variety of wants properly because of conflict and indecision, or suffering from strange fears and distorted wants which cloud our perceptions and warp our judgment. But advice about mental health and what is necessary for it is negative, limiting sort of advice. It does not tell us what wants are worth satisfying; it stipulates merely that there must be a degree of regulation and absence of conflict for any system of wants to be effectively satisfied, and lays down certain necessary conditions for this.

Advocates of 'growth' or 'self-actualization', however, explicitly go beyond the requirement of the satisfaction of basic needs and the limited, rather formal, requirements involved in the notion of rationality or 'mental health' so far outlined; and they write these additional recommendations into their account of 'mental health'. Maslow, for instance, distinguishes 'deficiency motivation' from 'growth motivation'. The former covers what I have called basic needs—biological needs together with those for love, security, etc.—which he regards as forms of 'tension reduction'. These are to be contrasted with 'self-actualization of potential capacities and talents, to devotion to a mission in life or a vocation, to activity rather than rest or resignation. A self-actualizing person experiences the maintenance of tension in these areas as pleasurable; he cannot be understood as being motivated here by the need for tension reduction. The greater the amount of growth motivation, the healthier a person is' (p. 33). Allport too maintains that 'By growth motives we refer to the hold that ideals gain upon the process of development.' It is connected with the extension of the self, with 'investment in living' and with growth and direction towards goals higher than the mere satisfaction of basic needs. Presumably, then, on this showing, a peasant living just above the subsistence level would be mentally unhealthy. He would have some practical shrewdness, perhaps, and some traditional system of values which would give him principles by reference to which he could regulate his wants. He would thus satisfy the third criterion of 'integration'. He would not, however, be 'self-actualizing' because I am postulating that he has no goals which are higher than the mere satisfaction of basic needs.

Now it is admirable enough to hold up such self-actualization as an ideal; though its justification is a difficult matter;[1] but it is odd to build it into a concept of 'mental health'. And does it not differ radically, in emphasis at any rate, from the criteria of the Freudian school, to mention only the classical exponents of the notion of 'mental health'? For, it might be argued, does not the Freudian take us farther than telling us what we must have if we are to satisfy and regulate any system of wants? Does he not also

[1] See R. S. Peters and A. P. Griffiths, 'The Autonomy of Prudence', *Mind*, April 1962.

intimate a more positive policy by suggesting that some wants are natural, whereas others are artificial, derivative, and hence unimportant in comparison with the natural ones? Sex, eating, drinking, he would hold, are fundamental to man in a way in which art and arithmetic are not. Wants, in other words, can be arranged in tiers, with the bottom level nearest to nature.

Whatever is meant by 'nature' in this account, it is really of little help even to a Freudian in deciding which wants are worth pursuing. For on this view scientific investigation itself, to whose ideals Freud himself was resolutely committed, is an 'unnatural activity'—a sublimation of infantile sexual curiosity or a method of reassuring himself against insecurity. Nevertheless he has to make judgments in which the time he is to give to science must be weighed against the rival attractions of food, sex, and the pursuit of power. The explanation which he gives of such activities may influence his judgment. A Freudian, for instance, would be unlikely to discount the claims of sex in the ways in which an artist or religious man might. But such a view of human nature would do little more than limit his judgments about what was worth doing. It would not provide positive counsels for his own life or for the education of his children.

In this respect a Freudian is in the same kind of boat as the rest of us. For, without going into any special theories, we can easily see how psychological considerations of this sort do little more than limit the range of our judgments. A man might have plenty of food, sex, drink and security—a pastoral life surrounded by the joys of the countryside. But when we spoke to him of the delicacies of human relationships, of art, of the excitement of discovery, he might spit and say that we needed our brains testing. From a psychological point of view he might be mentally healthy, integrated, adjusted—all of these things—but at the level of what Plato called 'the necessary appetites'. The Freudian can do little more than tell us that we neglect these at our peril; for he sees mental illness and neurosis as brought about by the ways in which such basic needs are thwarted or stunted. But his ideal of mental health is a negative one, to be defined against the absence of such deviations, distortions and conflicts. It is tantamount to the requirement that man should try to preserve his essential nature as a rational animal.

Those, however, who speak of 'growth' and 'self-actualization' explicitly go beyond these minimal requirements in their account of 'mental health'. And this is not very conducive to clarity; for though people may be missing a lot that they might find satisfying if they don't devote themselves to art, music and good causes, it is odd to describe them as mentally ill. It may, perhaps, be the case that in a highly complex and competitive society men may become mentally ill if they don't get absorbed in something or other above the level of the necessary appetites—even if it be in football or sailing rather than in the campaign for nuclear disarmament. But a condition necessary for mental health under certain social and economic circumstances should not be written into the meaning of 'mental health'.

The Role of the Educator

We have indeed reached the limit above which counsels about 'mental health' cease to have much application. For we have come to the point where Mill posed the contrast between the pig satisfied and Socrates dissatisfied. We have also, surely, come to the point where the psychologist leaves off and the educator takes over. For civilization is the constant endeavour of man to impose artifice on nature, to rise above the level of the necessary appetites. It involves the perpetuation of a whole mass of complicated activities which are worth doing for their own sake and which are not merely fuel for the glowing fire of our natural needs. The teacher is at the key-point in this constant endeavour of man to hand on these activities and the critical attitude necessary for their continuance and development. To hand on these activities properly is also to hand on the ideals and principles which are, as it were, immanent in them. To teach science *as* science, philosophy *as* philosophy, or history *as* history is to pass on respect for truth, argument and evidence; it is not simply to hand over a lot of information. These disciplines make explicit criteria by reference to which various forms of belief can be rationally assessed. The educator is therefore concerned in a positive manner with the maintenance and extension of rationality in fields which go far beyond beliefs which are necessary for the satisfaction of the necessary appetites. For the beliefs with which he is concerned are part and parcel of a quite different form of life.

But there are foolish and wise ways of handing on this thin crust of civilization, just as there are imaginative and dull ways of doing it. The psychologist cannot, *qua* psychologist, provide a justification of civilized activities, although his theorizing and practice as a psychologist is a pre-eminent example of a civilized activity; but what he can do is to warn teachers about foolish ways of passing on such activities. There are levels of development in childhood, and damage can be done if even the basic skills of reading, writing and arithmetic are passed on too early; there are ways, too, of teaching skills which may be damaging. And the importance of such skills can be emphasized with complete disregard for basic needs like those for love and security. Warped and stunted children may result from foolish methods of teaching. This is where talk of mental health, of integration, and of wholeness is relevant as a negative counsel of great importance. It is something that educators should never neglect while they educate people. But I have never been able to grasp how it could be thought that such counsels could ever provide positive ideals. For education is not a remedial business, unless one views life as something merely to be endured like an illness. The objection to talking of mental health as a unifying ideal for education is not simply, then, that it can at best be only a rather limited and negative counsel; it is also that it confuses the function of the educator in society with that of the doctor. The main function of the teacher is to train and instruct; it is not to help and cure.

While the educator is engaged in handing on the traditions, skills and activities which distinguish civilized life from that of the savages he must also be concerned with the development of rationality in a sense which is more basic than the development of critical standards by means of which highly sophisticated systems of belief can be assessed. He must be concerned with preserving the nature of man as a rational animal as covered by at least four of Jahoda's criteria of 'mental health'. Such an intelligent concern for the pupil as well as for the traditions of thought, the rules and the skills to be handed on has traditionally been referred to as the training of character and of the emotions. The former is concerned with rationality in the sense of helping children to impose plans and rules on their wants; the latter is concerned mainly with the development of objective standards of appraisal so that the child will come to view himself and the situations in which he is placed under aspects other than that of threat or what is wished for. The educator may also address himself to the task implicit in Jahoda's fourth criterion—the development of autonomy in the child, though little is known about how best this is done.[1] To speak of the teacher as being concerned with these

[1] See R. S. Peters, 'Freud's Theory of Moral Development in Relation to that of Piaget', *Brit. J. Educ. Psychol.*, Vol. XXX, Part III, Nov. 1960.

things as well as with the transmission of knowledge and skills is a salutary corrective to a one-sided approach to children. But it is much better to speak of these things in traditional terms than to speak of 'mental health'. For that confuses the image of the teacher's function in society. It is unnecessary and misleading to saddle the teacher with a remedial function by saying that 'mental health' should be one of his aims when what is covered by this term can be referred to in more traditional ways which do not carry the implication that the teacher is a special sort of doctor. This is not, of course, to say that there should not be experts readily available to whom the teacher can refer cases of breakdown; there are school doctors after all, and school dentists, so why not school psychiatrists? It is only to say that 'mental health' should not be regarded as an aim of an educator.

The cynic, of course, might reply that schools for many adolescents are in such a sorry state that there is little more that can be done than to have policemen in to stop riots, caretakers to keep the place clean, doctors and dentists to look after physical health and psychiatrically trained 'teachers' to care for the 'mental health' of the inmates. For the conditions of schooling and the attitudes of the inmates make any talk of 'education' as out of place as a fashion parade would be on a dung-hill. But the cynic here concedes the main point which I am trying to make; and it is questionable whether his counsel of despair is justified in the light of examples of what can be done by imaginative teachers with the most unlikely material in appalling circumstances. Education is so much a matter of confidence, of imagination, and of enthusiasm; and it has not got to take the form of initiating farm-workers into a love for Shakespeare and symphony concerts. The emphasis on 'mental health' reflects, amongst other things, a failure of nerve on the part of educators, a retreat from the positive.

Furthermore the reference to 'mental health' as an educational aim is yet another way of perpetuating the obnoxious view that education must have some aim beyond itself, that it must have some practical use in 'the outside world' or that it must be some sort of 'investment' which it is worthwhile for a community to spend money on. Presumably 'the outside world' refers to activities like business, government or running a home, which are 'life' in some sense in which devoting oneself to photography, philosophy or painting are not. Education, on this view, is all right if it helps a man to make money, to get on with his neighbours or with his wife; if it can't it must be an ivory-tower eccentricity advocated by egg-heads. Now though activities such as science may contribute to practical ends it is treason to civilization to see them only under such an aspect. For education is not just a *preparation* for 'living' in this sense; it is an initiation into a distinctive form of life. For an educated man is one who has an understanding of his own past, of literature and scientific discovery, and other practically 'useless' activities, which distinguish him from rats and savages. Such a man would agree that material things have to be produced, houses built, wars fought perhaps, and governmental tasks efficiently and fairly carried out. For these practical concerns are necessary for perpetuating those truly civilized activities which distinguish civilized men from savages. Indeed much of the study of history, literature and philosophy is concerned with the evaluation, criticism and suggested improvement of ways of living. One of the diseases of contemporary thought about education is its preoccupation with the practical, with the mechanics of life, to the exclusion of concern about what sort of life is worth living.

It can be argued that such disciplines of thought and feeling have a practical function in so far as they constitute some general requirements for citizenship in a democracy. For such a society is a formal façade unless it is peopled by men and women who understand their own past and who can think critically and with understanding about current problems. There is some truth in this; but it has to be stated more cautiously. In the first place the democratic way of life, in so far as it embodies principles like equality, justice and liberty, is an articulation in a social context of 'rationality' in some of the senses already distinguished.[1] And this way of life, in so far as it can approximate under modern conditions to the Athenian polis, might be regarded as valuable in itself. But it might also be regarded as instrumentally valuable in that it is necessary, in so far as it provides conditions of security and non-interference, for other pursuits that are worth while in themselves. This was Spinoza's defence of democracy. This point can be illustrated by the story of the philosopher who was upbraided by the Marxist for only being concerned to understand the world and not to change it. The philosopher asked the Marxist what people were going to do when the classless society had been attained. To the admission by the Marxist that people might then get round to more theoretical pursuits like philosophy, the philosopher replied 'Maybe I am ahead of my time, then.'

In the second place disciplines like history and literature are debased and distorted if they are used consciously to inculcate 'critical thinking' and sensitivity. Such habits of mind may in fact develop if people enter imaginatively into philosophy, history and literature and come to appreciate what they are from the inside. They must care about the problems there presented and must come to appreciate things like the cogency of arguments, the elegance of proofs, the inevitability of events. But they can only do this from the inside. Without this initiation into the activity, 'critical

[1] See S. I. Benn and R. S. Peters, *Social Principles and the Democratic State*, Allen & Unwin, 1960, *passim*.

88

thinking', sensitivity and so on become superficial second-hand things, a gloss which enables people to talk at parties, not structures built deeply into their minds. And the disciplines themselves become distorted and mangled. Indeed the classics may come to appear only in books of 'Readings'!

Whether an activity is practical or not depends on the aspect under which it is viewed. Both science and carpentry can be viewed as instrumental to something else or they can be valued for what they are, for the extent to which they come up to their own intrinsic standards of excellence. For many people the delights of history, science and literature are difficult to appreciate. But there are civilized delights in simpler skills which are attainable by most men. The question is whether things are done mainly because they contribute to extrinsic ends such as money or prestige or whether they are delighted in for their own sake. And, of course, many activities are and must be regarded under both aspects. The preoccupation with the practical is the tendency to look on activities only under a means–end aspect.

In the struggle to develop a civilized form of life many have become mentally ill, and many of the great advances in civilization have been made by men who were patently mentally ill. So what? Does this detract from the value of their efforts? Surely not. It shows however that what is called 'self-actualization' is often pursued at a cost. And if some enthusiastic educators, who really understand what education is about, sometimes push their pupils too hard and forget that they have emotions to control, a love-life to lead, and a 'living' to be earned, it may be salutary to remind them of this from time to time. But this is better done by speaking of this in terms of vocational training, of the training of the emotions and of character. For such old-fashioned ideals did at least not confuse the task of the educator with that of the doctor. They did at least imply that children were to be treated as responsible agents worthy to carry on the activities of a civilized community; they did not imply, as does the stress on mental health, that children are to be treated as patients who have to be weaned in a kindly way to nibble at the raw meat of the modern world.

V

THE PROBLEM OF VALUES AND JOHN DEWEY

by

T. H. B. HOLLINS

'The tigers of wrath are wiser than the horses of instruction,' says Blake. This is an example of a value-judgment in education. It is a difficult one, not only because of its gnomic form, but because we should have to arrive at a standard for judging wisdom before agreeing or disagreeing. The teacher is working in a situation where many decisions about values have been taken before he begins teaching, e.g. that schooling is of value, that a certain curriculum is the best; but he himself cannot take a lesson without making many choices; the teacher of history, for instance, may have to decide whether to present Napoleon or Cromwell as admirable or despicable or both. All these judgments are characterized by the making of difficult choices on inconclusive evidence (in so far as the teacher is conscious of the need for choice); they are the 'open questions' with which the philosophy of education is particularly concerned. The fundamental problem for the philosophically inclined teacher is whether there is not one ultimate value (or perhaps a few values) which, if we could find and define, would give us a standard by which to judge all minor values; in short, can we locate and define the Beautiful and the Good? In order to discuss this question, I have chosen to talk about the philosophy of John Dewey, who came to the conclusion that there was no hierarchy of values and no *summum bonum*.

John Dewey was born in 1859 and although he lived until 1952, he was a typical nineteenth-century figure. His thinking was particularly influenced by Hegel (against whom he reacted strongly) and Darwin. From both he got the idea of a world constantly changing; like Hegel he saw the 'social' as a category of existence and explanation; and from Darwin he obtained the picture of man as a part of nature, engaged in a long transaction with its forces and learning gradually to control them. His philosophy then is set in a biological and social matrix. From this matrix comes his theory of experience. 'Nature' and 'experience' are difficult words which have been used in so many ways in philosophy that they are now almost vacuous. Dewey never defines them in his major philosophical work *Experience and Nature*; in any case he is sometimes as obscure as Hegel in his writing. 'Nature' apparently means 'the collective phenomena of the world', but to this definition must be added man and his experiences; this differs from many philosophies, where man and experience stand in part outside nature and transcend it. As nature is always in flux, phenomena must be thought of as 'events' rather than 'objects'. Experience seems to be in two stages: primary experience, consisting of 'gross, macroscopic, crude subject-matter', which is 'had' before it is cognized: and a refined, derived experience which is obtained by intelligence working on the primary: this refined experience gives 'knowledge' which in turn gives the possibility of control of the environment. So far we have a picture of the individual experiencing the phenomena of nature. To it must be added experience which comes through communication with other men; this is of the greatest importance, as the 'social' is a major category in Dewey's philosophy. 'Shared experience is the greatest of human goods.'[1] Man is the most successful animal because

[1] *Experience and Nature*, p. 202.

he has learnt to think and communicate in symbols; symbols gain meaning by use in social situations; 'the use of language to convey and acquire ideas is an extension and refinement of the principle that things gain meaning by being used in a shared experience or joint action';[1] 'to be really members of a social group is therefore to attach the same meanings to things and to acts which others attach'.[2] Social experience reconstructs personality. 'Individuals who are not bound together in associations, whether domestic, economic, religious, political, artistic, or educational, are monstrosities. It is absurd to suppose that the ties which hold them together are merely external and do not react into mentality and character, producing the framework of personal disposition.'[3] Mind itself is a social product; 'mind represents the whole general system of meanings'.[4] Experience, especially social experience, is a constantly recurring theme in Dewey's theory of educational values: in fact he defines education as 'that reconstruction or reorganization of experience which adds to the meaning of experience, and which increases ability to direct the course of subsequent experience'.[5]

Let us now look at Dewey's theory of knowledge, with its setting—'the problematic situation', and the method of obtaining it—'the theory of inquiry', both essential for an understanding of his thinking about values. To a nineteenth-century Darwinian, considering man's evolution, the most important kind of knowledge would be practical knowledge, giving increased control of natural forces, including those forces within man himself which are inimical to civilization. This is Dewey's position. The best kind of thinking, which

[1] *Democracy and Education*, p. 19.   [2] Ibid., p. 36.
[3] *Individualism, Old and New*, pp. 81, 82.
[4] *Experience and Nature*, p. 303.
[5] *Democracy and Education*, pp. 89, 90.

he calls 'reflection' or 'inquiry', would be that which arises in problematic situations and helps to solve problems; thinking is encouraged and a solution sought with more determination if the problem is one which arises in a man's own experience. Inquiry is generalized into the method which is used to convert primary experience into the refined experience called knowledge: it is 'the controlled or directed transformation of an indeterminate situation into one that is so determinate in its constituent distinctions and relations as to convert the elements of the original situation into a unified whole'.[1] Ideas are tools or instruments used in the process of inquiry; hence the name 'instrumentalism' which Dewey gives to his own version of pragmatism (pragmatism being (i) a doctrine which estimates any assertion by its practical bearing on human interests, (ii) a method for determining the truth of an assertion by an examination of consequences which follow from it). Knowledge is not to be thought of in an absolute way; it is to be used in further inquiries and may be transformed in the process. The test of truth is verification: 'in physical matters men have slowly grown accustomed in all specific beliefs to identifying the true with the verified. But they still hesitate to recognize the implication of this identification and to derive the definition of truth from it.'[2] This quotation gives us the clue as to what kind of knowledge is most admired by Dewey and the model to which all knowledge should approximate; it is, of course, the secure, tested knowledge of the physical sciences. Dewey's method of inquiry and reflective thought is a simplified version of scientific method. Whether most scientific thinking begins in a 'problematic situation' is very doubtful, but it has been a fertile idea for 'progressive' education. *How We Think*, a book in which Dewey sets out the

[1] *Logic: The Theory of Inquiry*, pp. 104–5.
[2] *Reconstruction in Philosophy*, p. 159.

method of reflection for education, remains the best theoretical basis for 'activity methods' and project work. As we shall see, the 'problematic situation' is a central concept for understanding Dewey's theory of values. At this point it is enough to see its importance in his theory of knowledge: 'the problematic situation is *the* context in which everything I say about knowing is placed and by reference to which it is to be understood'.[1] Everyone knows the homely illustration in *How We Think*,[2] of the man who comes to a branching in the road and who has now to think out the answer to the problem as to which road to take, and the familiar yet striking sentence which concludes the story—'Thinking begins in . . . a *forked-road* situation.'

It is not my intention to examine the detailed educational theory which Dewey draws from this philosophical position, as I wish to discuss values in a general way. But I should like to make a few generalizations characterizing his theory of education, in order to make my first point about values, an obvious one, that they may depend on philosophical positions or systems. As values are not fixed and it is hoped that the next generation will find better solutions to their problems than we have done, Dewey's ideal school is not one in which teachers impose their values, but one in which the teacher arranges situations and materials (naturally using his own values as a guide) and encourages the child to arrive at his own solutions by problem-solving and critical appraisal. Curricula are thought of in terms of problems to be solved rather than subject-areas to be studied; this means that problems of science and social studies are likely to be given more weight than art or music. As the best knowledge is practical, first-hand experience is given preference over book-learning, especially in the early years. Values being tentative and the reconstruction of experience having no definite direction,

[1] *Experience, Knowledge and Value.*   [2] pp. 13–14.

the child rather than the subject-matter takes the centre of the stage. Finally, and most important, the school must be 'a genuine form of active community life instead of a place set apart in which to learn lessons'. I think these educational considerations do follow from Dewey's philosophy of experience. On the other hand, and this is my second point about values, they do not follow of necessity; that is, there is no logical entailment. Many people have agreed with Dewey's educational programme, while rejecting his philosophy. Jacques Maritain, for instance, a well-known Neo-Thomist educationist, often writes with approval of Dewey's educational theory. What we have is a kind of loose dependence of educational values on theories about the nature of man or the universe.

Before proceeding to Dewey's ideas about values, it is necessary to get a clearer perspective, by bringing forward some of the more serious criticisms which have been made of Dewey's philosophy. Two of the weightiest can be summed up in these quotations from Santayana's review of Dewey's *Experience and Nature*:

(i) ... How comes it that Dewey has a metaphysics of his own, that cosmology is absent from his system, and that every natural fact becomes in his hands so strangely unseizable and perplexing? This question, which is the crux of the whole system, may be answered, I think, in a single phrase: *the dominance of the foreground*.

(ii) In Dewey, ... there is a pervasive, quasi-Hegelian tendency to dissolve the individual into his social functions.

The phrase, the 'dominance of the foreground', serves to remind us how one-sided Dewey's view of life is. His insistence on solving present problems, on the value of the practical, on active experience, on change, is eloquent and salutary, but may lead us to overlook the value of contemplation, of experiences which are 'received' and enjoyed for their own sake, especially the aesthetic, and of the value of tradition, of 'the best which has been thought and said in the world'. The second quotation attacks Dewey's preoccupation with the social side of experience; he undervalues the individual's need for a strong inner-life of his own. Consider the implications, for instance, of this passage from *Democracy and Education*.[1]

And the idea of perfecting an 'inner' personality is a sure sign of social divisions. What is called inner is simply that which does not connect with others—which is not capable of free and full communication. What is termed spiritual culture has usually been futile, with something rotten about it, just because it has been conceived as a thing which a man might have internally—and therefore exclusively. What one is as a person is what one is as associated with others, in a free give and take of intercourse.

G. H. Bantock, in his swingeing attack on Dewey in the *Cambridge Review* for June 1952, points out the danger of such a view; it preaches a kind of social conformism which is but a short step to McCarthyism. Bantock also points out a possible weakness in Dewey's theory of problem-solving —that in most fields people need to have a thorough grounding in knowledge which may not be immediately useful, or even interesting, before they begin to recognize problems at all.

Further criticism can now be made in considering Dewey's theory of values in more detail. Dewey does not differentiate between the status of empirical, e.g. scientific, statements and value statements. Like all other knowledge, values arise in problematic situations, they are clarified by inquiry, and are tested by verification. For instance, on the most important of value-judgments, moral laws, he says: 'A moral

[1] p. 143.

based on study of human nature instead of upon disregard for it would find the facts of man continuous with those of the rest of nature and would thereby ally ethics with physics or biology.'[1] Now recent analytical philosophy has gone some way towards clearing up confusions about the status of different sorts of propositions. An empirical statement such as 'the earth is round' can be shown to be true or false; a weakened form of the verification principle is used, i.e. that tests can be thought out and agreed on by those competent to know which will settle the question. But a value-judgment, such as 'Stealing is wrong', although it has the same grammatical form as 'the earth is round', has a different logical status. The true/false criterion does not apply and it is always possible for moralists to agree or disagree with the pronouncement. This does not mean, however, that evidence is unimportant in making the decision to agree or disagree. A value-judgment contains three elements: (i) the implication of personal approval—I approve of this, (ii) a prescriptive element—you would be wise to think as I do, and (iii) an implied standard for making the judgment—it is here that facts have a place in providing evidence for the view that is held. This position follows from the famous observation of Hume that 'ought' statements cannot be deduced from 'is' statements. Nowell-Smith in his *Ethics* gives a good example. He quotes Bishop Mortimer: 'The first foundation is the doctrine of God the Creator. God made us and all the world. *Because of that* He has an absolute claim on our obedience. We do not exist in our own right, but only as His creatures, who ought *therefore* to do and be what He desires.' Nowell-Smith comments, 'This argument requires the premise that a creature ought to obey his creator, which is itself a moral judgment.' I have time only for this summary statement. If the argument is convincing,

[1] *Human Nature and Conduct*, p. 12.

it means that Dewey is wrong on this point and that teachers will look in vain for an authority which can settle the truth or falsity of some of the difficult judgments they have to make. It can be seen that this is also a theoretical justification for the statement made earlier that Dewey's educational theory is not necessarily entailed by his philosophy of nature. Statements about the nature of the world or of man are 'is' statements; value-judgments, e.g. prescriptions for educational practice, are 'ought' statements, and cannot follow logically from 'is' statements. Even more important, we can see that the quest for an ultimate Good is doomed to failure; the adjective 'good' has descriptive, commendatory and prescriptive elements and because of the commendatory and prescriptive elements it always makes sense to say of any chosen ultimate Good—'is it really good?', which would be nonsensical if 'good' were purely descriptive, like 'green'.

Dewey is at one with the analytical philosophers in believing that no ultimate good can be found which will set a standard for lesser goods. On morals he says 'Ethical theory has been singularly hypnotized by the notion that its business is to discover some final end or good or some ultimate and supreme law . . .' May we not 'advance to a belief in the plurality of changing, moving, individualized goods and ends, and to a belief that principles, criteria, laws are intellectual instruments for analysing individual or unique situations?'[1] Dewey may be right in thinking that every moral situation is unique, and therefore the possible immediate consequences must always play a part in determining the course of action, but he stresses these consequences too much and does not allow enough for the fairly stable standards we also apply in any unique situation. 'Philosophic criticism . . . has to appraise values by taking cognizance of

[1] *Reconstruction in Philosophy*, pp. 161, 162.

their causes and consequences.'[1] This is characteristic of Dewey on values. Only grudgingly does he admit the existence of standards and then only as tools which may suggest new responses.

. . . A multitude of generalized ends are acknowledged as goods. But the *value* of this systematization is intellectual or analytic. Classifications *suggest* possible traits to be on the look-out for in studying a particular case; they suggest methods of action to be tried in removing the inferred causes of ill. They are tools of insight; their value is in promoting an individualized response in the individual situation.[2]

Yet most of us will think these standards or 'classifications' of goods do more than suggest; that they may in fact be the determinants of decisions. To take an example. Suppose a young teacher has been brought up to believe that it is wrong to use physical force against anyone. He begins to teach in a 'tough' secondary school and soon has such trouble with discipline that his class is out of hand. He observes that his colleagues control the class by a sparing but effective use of corporal punishment. He begins to consider whether he should not do the same. A consideration of 'consequences' suggest that such action will be effective. He not only has the example of his colleagues but perhaps, being only a young teacher and having only just left college, he is still interested in educational theory, and he is convinced by Professor Eysenck's paper in the *British Journal of Educational Psychology* for February 1960 that moral education is synonymous with 'conditioning', and, as Eysenck says, 'the maxim "spare the rod, spoil the child" could with advantage, be applied to the extraverted, possibly psychopathic, non-conditioner, whereas the modern free-and-easy methods of

[1] *Experience and Nature*, p. 408.
[2] *Reconstruction in Philosophy*, p. 169.

upbringing would be much more appropriate to the intro-verted, anxious, easy-to-condition type of child'. One thing our teacher is certain of is that the ringleaders of disorder are 'extraverted non-conditioners' and probably psychopathic. Will he take to the strap? Probably he will when he becomes desperate, but only for reasons of expediency and not because he thinks it's right. And this is because he is not only an 'introverted conditioner' himself, who naturally chooses 'progressive' methods, but because he has a standard of behaviour which is of a higher order and more determinant of conduct than a consideration of immediate consequences.

It may now seem that I am contradicting myself. On the one hand, I am approving of Dewey's rejection of the *summum bonum*; on the other hand, I am disapproving of his insistence on immediate consequences and the multiplicity of ends, and saying that higher standards are important; and if there are *higher* standards, why not a *highest*? I do want to maintain both positions, however. I believe that standards can be arranged in a hierarchy. To make use of (and alter) an example from R. M. Hare's *The Language of Morals*: when we were young we were taught the moral rule 'Do not say what is false'; but a war comes along and we then agree perhaps to revise this rule to—'Do not say what is false, except to the enemy.' Why? Presumably because we thought we were fighting in a just war; one aim in defeating Hitler was to stop the mass extermination of the Jews and other minorities; we could therefore alter our rule to 'Do not say what is false, except to save lives'. My hierarchy here is (i) saving life, (ii) winning a just war is important, (iii) do not tell lies. But it is still open for another moralist to say 'Never say what is false, because the truth is even more im-portant than saving lives'; so suggesting a different kind of hierarchy. The moral rules at the top of the hierarchy can always be challenged, as I said earlier. Perhaps it might be agreed that the rules near this mysterious summit are all concerned with treating human beings as 'persons' (to use the fashionable existentialist word); moral rules such as 'Love your neighbour as yourself' and 'Love your enemies' are obviously highly generalized standards of conduct which most of us, in our better moments, would try to apply in innumerable special situations calling for a judgment of value. Hare gives us a hint that the only way to justify our standards is to justify our whole way of life.

If it is agreed that 'standards' are more important than 'consequences' (to speak loosely, because they merge into each other) and that there are hierarchies of standards, two further criticisms can be made of Dewey's theory of values. The first is that Dewey is mistaken in stressing 'the changing, moving, individualized' nature of 'goods and ends' (though this is important to him for his Theory of Inquiry). Moral rules, for instance, as we have just seen, are highly generalized, and most of them have hardly changed in two thousand years. Again the 'philosophy of the foreground' is at fault. I am, of course, allying myself with Dewey in advocating a relativist theory of values (which will be anathema to those who believe in absolute values), but there are degrees of stability in the relativist position. The second criticism turns on the belief that if you reject stable and lasting 'goods' and standards, you ought not to use terms which suggest grading and choice, like 'better' and 'best'. But judgments of value cannot be made and a philosophy cannot be expressed without them. Now it is noticeable how often Dewey uses such terms. Consider a quotation given earlier—'shared experience is the greatest of human goods'. 'Greatest' and 'goods' suggest comparison, choice, a hierarchy of standards: the framework of choice needs to be made explicit: is the 'shared experience' of thieves valuable? Was 'shared experience' in the Hitler youth movement valuable? Clearly, ends which are outside 'shared experience' have to be brought in. Therefore Dewey is commonly criticized for not making his aims and standards explicit and for making so many statements where his aims have to be guessed at.

It is, of course, necessary for Dewey's theory of experience and inquiry that aims in education should not be insisted on. As, in some sense, standards are always to be made, it is impossible to state what they are now. But he might well have given more attention to a statement of tentative positive aims. This he refused to do; he thought he should limit himself to a critique of the weaknesses in education:

And we do not emphasize things which do not require emphasis —that is, such things as are taking care of themselves fairly well. We tend rather to frame our statement on the basis of the defects and needs of the contemporary situation; we take for granted, without explicit statement which would be of no use, whatever is right or approximately so. We frame our explicit aims in terms of some alteration to be brought about.[1]

The critic immediately asks 'alteration in what direction?' which requires an answer in terms of positive aims. The one aim Dewey would allow was that good education was that which allowed the child continued growth; bad education would limit growth in one or more directions and dry up the desire for education: 'since in reality there is nothing to which growth is relative save more growth, there is nothing to which education is subordinate save more education'.[2] This is not sensible. Dandelions do far better, in the absence of control, than roses; they are more biologically successful; but we don't encourage them for this reason. Growth in children has to be in a socially desirable direction.

It is, in fact, necessary with Dewey to make explicit the

[1] *Democracy and Education*, p. 130.
[2] Ibid., p. 60.

aims he assumes; and 'growth in a socially desirable direction' is the main one. It would be unfair to him to say he never recognizes this. In *Democracy and Education* he says, 'The conception of education as a social process and function has no definite meaning until we define the kind of society we have in mind' (p. 112), and in *Experience and Education* he adds 'democracy is the best of all social institutions'. But his critique of democracy is remarkably thin and weak; in quantity alone it occupies very few pages in *Democracy and Education*. He stresses the need for equality of opportunity (without examining notions of equality) and the value of knowledge to the citizen; he is rather good on the need for diversity within a democracy and to have power widely distributed; but this is not discussed in relation to an ideal put forward in another essay that we should have a planned society with close control of production. And when we look for a more philosophical discussion of what democracy entails we are back where we started, with the 'principles of growth':

Democracy has many meanings, but if it has a moral meaning, it is found in resolving that the supreme test of all political institutions and industrial arrangements shall be the contribution they make to the all-round growth of every member of society.[1]

The possible weaknesses of democracy, summed up in such phrases as 'the tyranny of the majority' and 'minority culture in a mass civilization', the saddening thought that schools spend so much of their time fighting against democratic values of the Admass type, hardly engage Dewey's attention. He does say 'it is the business of the school environment to eliminate, as far as possible, the unworthy features of the existing environment',[2] but he seems to be thinking of such

[1] *Reconstruction in Philosophy*, p. 186.
[2] *Democracy and Education*, p. 24.

features as crime rather than, say, 'keeping up with the Jones's' or the power of the advertiser. Dewey's view of democracy is uncritical, too comfortable, like his view of man and the universe; one cannot imagine him sympathizing with Donne's 'Batter my heart, three-person'd God' or with Yeats' 'Now that my ladder's gone, I must lie down where all the ladders start, in the foul rag-and-bone shop of the heart.' But I am going too far; a reasonable optimism in man's chances of living in a satisfactory world is unfashionable but not incomprehensible or contemptible. A passage like the following from *Experience and Nature*,[1] though over-written, is not without nobility.

Men move between extremes. They conceive of themselves as gods, or feign a powerful and cunning god as an ally who bends the world to do their bidding and meet their wishes. Disillusionized, they disown the world that disappoints them; and hugging ideals to themselves as their own possessions, stand in haughty aloofness apart from the hard course of events that pays so little heed to our hopes and aspirations. But a mind that has opened itself to experience and that has ripened through its discipline knows its own littleness and impotences; it knows that its wishes and acknowledgments are not final measures of the universe whether in knowledge or in conduct, and hence are, in the end, transient. But it also knows that its juvenile assumption of power and achievement is not a dream to be wholly forgotten. . . . A chastened sense of our importance, apprehension that it is not a yard-stick by which to measure the whole, is consistent with the belief that we and our endeavours are significant not only for themselves but in the whole.

I have got away from Dewey's theory of values, but it seemed important to show that the unsatisfactory nature of the theory, when it comes to the question of standards, led to unsatisfactory results in Dewey's own thinking about

[1] p. 419.

aims in education. 'Weak in aims, strong in method', is the usual, and convincing, charge made against the naturalist philosophers. Rousseau's phrases, e.g. 'No book but the world': 'let him not be taught science, let him discover it' are echoed in Dewey's educational pronouncements; echoed in less graceful language, but given a contemporary framework; the practice worked out afresh after a century's development of science, industrialism and universal education. Yet to say that Dewey is strong in method is not to say that his theory of values is negligible. For firstly the development of the spirit of inquiry, of 'critical intelligence', in the young, is itself a very important educational aim. Secondly, the recognition that even the highest values are not immutable will make teachers see the urgency, as never before, of developing in children both a sense of responsibility for not lightly questioning accepted values, and yet a courageous independence, so that when they do question, they are determined to hold fast to what they find good.

For educational values, Dewey's method emphasizes (i) the need for children to learn *practically* about values, (ii) the need for them to make choices of their own, based on (iii) a study, conducted in the spirit of scientific inquiry, of the possible consequences of choice (and from these three to develop critical powers), (iv) a consideration by the teacher of the age and intelligence of the children to be taught; so that the problems are meaningful to them, and (v) the need for children to learn about values in co-operation with others. We, more concerned about the character of the goal than the best ways of running to it, would add to them (vi) a consideration of the standards of values; are these standards themselves the best? We might also be concerned with the need for children to acquire information before making choices, but the follower of Dewey might reasonably reply that this should be acquired as the child's interest develops during practice. A decision about what values are most important will decide what subject-matter should be given preference in the curriculum (with the proviso that good teachers are more important than good subjects). Dewey rejects this, of course: 'We cannot establish a hierarchy of values among studies':[1] but if there is a hierarchy of values and, as most people think, moral values are the most important, pride of place in the curriculum will have to be given to English literature, history and religion, and, at the university, to other humane disciplines. Our usual grammar school curriculum can, in fact, be justified in this way (except that the past may figure too much in the material; the 'foreground' should not dominate, but how often does it appear at all?). But would not a teacher well versed in Dewey's doctrines think that some improvement could be made in method, by cutting down on the imparting of information and stereotyped attitudes, and lessening the domination of the pupil by the teacher? No wonder we can sometimes recognize teachers outside school: they are so used to teaching on the assumption that 'what I say three times is right' that didacticism becomes habitual. There should be more free discussion of values amongst the children. And there should be more provision for activities which allow children to learn the social virtues for themselves; can one pretend that the prefect system is enough?

There is finally the difficult question of how far one should encourage children to be critical of the very bases of society: to follow to the bitter end the spirit of inquiry. Most teachers would say that nothing but good can come from teaching children to be critical of the values I referred to earlier as Admass values. But shall we encourage them to question their religion or the accepted moral rules? It is noticeable that Plato kept his Guardians on mathematics

[1] *Democracy and Education*, p. 281.

and science when they were young and they were to be at least fifty before they studied dialectic, 'which is the ability to see the connexions of things'.[1] Lord James has an admirable discussion of the whole question in his pamphlet *Education and the Moral Basis of Citizenship*, but is he optimistic in thinking such a study can begin in the sixth form? Certainly a formal study, such as the root-and-branch analysis of modern philosophy, could not be undertaken before, and at a lesser level of intelligence. Our fear is that we might destroy belief and that nothing will take its place. But are we not faced with the situation that many children about to leave secondary modern schools take it as a matter of fact that some of the 'accepted' moral rules are not acceptable to them? It is therefore urgent that morals should be discussed sympathetically in such schools. Most teachers would do this responsibly, conscious of the need to be positive, following Aquinas: 'Do not dig a pit in front of your students, unless you are prepared to fill it up.' John Dewey would have the students filling in the pit, and not the teacher, but he too never doubts that it has to be filled.

[1] *Republic*, VII, 537.

VI

AIMS IN EDUCATION:
NEO-THOMISM

by

THE MOST REV. GEORGE ANDREW BECK

I

A GRAMMARIAN would probably say that, in describing man, we tend, in the present age, to concentrate on the adjectival rather than the substantive part of our definition. We can discuss primitive man, or medieval man, or western man, or economic man or psychological man, but we find it difficult enough to define man *tout court*. Yet the question of what man is—or what we mean by human nature—is the source of all social philosophy, and is ultimately the basis of every system of education. Only when we know what man is can we say what he should strive for, what sort of society he should live in, what institutions should serve him. Only when we know what man is can we say how he should be educated. Is man a glorified animal, expendable in the service of others, or in the service of the State; a part only of the whole, and subject to the whole? Is he to be trained in the skills and techniques of production and scientific achievement, a sort of human computer or automaton; and must economic aims be the overriding interest in education? Or is man a person with a rational spiritual nature, destined for immortality, with an importance transcending that of any other element in the universe—an end in himself with an eternal destiny? Is there a real distinction between right and wrong, and does it matter to himself and others what things a man chooses to do?

All these questions are intimately linked with the process and aims of education; all of them need an answer if the aims of education are to be defined.

Education, therefore, cannot escape the entanglements of philosophy and every educational system is a reflection of an attitude to, and a philosophy of, life which answers in some form or other the question 'What is man?'

Among the philosophies which seek to give an adequate and coherent account of the nature of man, the system of St. Thomas Aquinas occupies an important place. It is true that the Thomist system was given its expression in the second half of the thirteenth century and might easily be considered antiquated and possibly outmoded. It was the achievement of a young Neapolitan friar of good family—that of the Counts of Aquino—born at Roccasecca in 1225, professed as a Dominican friar at Paris in 1245, who commented and lectured chiefly in the University of Paris, but also in Orvieto and Rome from 1252 to 1272 before being sent to Naples, going to his death in 1274 at Fossa Nuova on his way back from the General Council of Lyons, on March 7, 1274.

Students and followers of St. Thomas have not experienced any insuperable difficulties in applying his thought and system to the world of modern scientific discovery, or to the more complex social patterns of twentieth-century society. Maritain, Gilson, Grabmann, Gemelli, Copleston, Hawkins, Noël, Phelan, Rooney and Lonergan are names not unknown among the modern philosophers, and the Neo-Thomist publications from Paris, Louvain, Milan, Toronto, the United States, and other centres of Neo-Thomist thought are evidence of the vitality of the rethought and Christianized Aristotelianism of the thirteenth-century Dominican friar.[1]

II

I am to speak on the educational aims of Neo-Thomism, and I venture to begin by a short account of Thomism as a philosophical system and of its bearing on education. May I attempt to remove a misunderstanding? It is sometimes said that the Thomist philosophy is an outmoded system based on the Aristotelian categories imposed arbitrarily on Catholics by authority of the Roman Church, whose theological dogmas would be undermined were the scholastic philosophy abandoned.

While it is true that the Thomist expression of reality is congenial to the Catholic Faith, it should be clear to anyone who has read the writings of Aquinas or of any modern Thomist that this system of philosophy in no way derives its principles from religious faith or from the authority of the Catholic Church. It is a philosophy based solely on experience, and living by reason. It is not limited to the ecclesiastical student or the theological college. There are a number of Neo-Thomists who are not Roman Catholics. It claims its place with the other sciences, with sociology,

[1] For a short survey of the Neo-Thomist movement since the publication of Pope Leo XIII's Encyclical Letter *Aeterni Patris* in August 1879 see, for example, F. J. Thonnard, *A Short History of Philosophy* and the bibliography given at the beginning of the Chapter entitled 'Neo-Thomism', p. 991. Among periodicals may be mentioned, *Angelicum* (Rome); *Divus Thomas* (Freiburg); *Laval Théologique et Philosophique* (Quebec); *The Modern Schoolman* (St. Louis, Missouri); *The New Scholasticism* (Washington); *Rivista di filosofia neo-scolastica* (Milan); *Revue néoscolastique de philosophie* (Louvain); *Revue Thomiste* (Saint-Maximin, Var); *The Thomist* (Washington).

politics, economics and ethnology as one of the instruments of human culture.[1]

What Catholics hold about the Thomist system is that it provides a rational account of man, his activities, his potentialities, his destiny, which not only is not in conflict with the truths made known by divine revelation, but helps to give them coherence and deeper meaning. The same system of thought applied to the data of divine revelation provides the texture of Thomist theology. It is true that the borderland between the two disciplines is not always clearly defined, but I venture to suggest that this is true of life itself. Truth cannot contradict truth without destroying the very first principle of human reason. Philosophy, independent of revelation, maintains the autonomy of human reason, but it is subject in a negative sense to the guidance of Faith by which its conclusions can be checked. The Church com-

[1] Father Copleston notes acutely that one might have expected St. Thomas as a Christian, a theologian and a friar to place the interior life and the soul's relation to God in the foreground of his philosophy, as was done, for example, by St. Bonaventure. 'In point of fact, however, one of the chief characteristics of St. Thomas's philosophy is its "objectivity" rather than its "subjectivity". The immediate object of the human intellect is the essence of the material thing, and St. Thomas builds up his philosophy by reflection on sense-experience. In the proofs which he gives of God's existence the process of argument is always from the sensible world to God. No doubt certain of the proofs could be applied to the soul itself as a starting-point and be developed in a different way; but in actual fact this was not the way of St. Thomas, and the proof which he calls the *via manifestior* is the one which is most dependent on Aristotle's own arguments. This Aristotelian "objectivity" of St. Thomas may appear disconcerting to those for whom "truth is subjectivity"; but at the same time it is a great source of strength, since it means that his arguments can be considered in themselves, apart from St. Thomas's own life, on their own merits or demerits, and that observations about "wishful thinking" are largely irrelevant, the relevant question being the objective cogency of the arguments themselves.' Frederick Copleston, S.J., *A History of Philosophy*, Vol. 2, p. 309.

mends the Thomist philosophy because its conclusions are in harmony with, and help to explain, the revealed truth of which she claims to be the guardian and interpreter.

Of the writings of Aquinas, the most important for our purpose are the two great summaries of his teaching: the *Summa contra Gentiles*, written in 1259 or 1260, and the *Summa Theologica* which was begun about 1260 and left uncompleted at his death in 1274. The only formal educational treatise which he wrote is a little tract called *De Magistro*, which discusses the question how a man learns, and was written about 1256.

The *Summa contra Gentiles* is a condensed piece of apologetic directed against the philosophers of Islam who shared common ground with Aquinas in accepting the philosophy of Aristotle. It is divided into four books, the first of which deals with God, the second with creatures, the third with happiness as the end or purpose of creation and the means of achieving happiness, and the fourth explaining the Christian mysteries—Trinity, Incarnation, the Sacraments, and how these revealed doctrines accord with human reason.

The *Summa Theologica* is St. Thomas's greatest work. It has been described as 'an educational document of the highest importance because it sets out a complete philosophy of man stating who and what he is, putting him in his setting and his relationship with all other being, declaring his purpose in life, and asserting how it must be achieved'.[1]

The treatise is divided into three parts, of which the second has two sub-divisions. The first part—the *prima pars* as

[1] See the contribution on 'Neo-Thomism' by Fr. W. Lawson, S.J., in *Education and the Philosophic Mind*, edited by A. V. Judges, London, Harrap, 1957, p. 45. The *Summa Theologica* has been translated into English by the Dominican Fathers. A remarkable French edition *Saint Thomas d'Aquin Somme Théologique* with valuable notes and explanations is being published in a series of small paperback volumes by the French Dominican *Revue des Jeunes*, Paris, Desclée et Cie.

Thomists call it—deals with the existence and nature of God, and with God as the first principle of things, going on to creation, the creation of the corporeal world, of man, the human soul, and the general government of the world by God. The second part is concerned with human conduct and I shall return to it in a moment. The third part deals with the economy of the Incarnation and the Redemption of man by Christ, its historical realization and the distribution of its effects through the sacramental system.

Although St. Thomas has a theory of knowledge and traces the steps by which man arrives at certitude in the possession of truth, he does not begin (as a reader acquainted with modern philosophy might expect) with a justification of metaphysics or the possibility of metaphysical knowledge. The defence of metaphysics has been left to the Neo-Thomists not only against Kant and the phenomenalists, but also against the logical positivists.

It has recently been the custom in English philosophical circles to say that problems of philosophy are no more than problems of language, and we must recognize that the logical positivists and neo-positivists have helped most of us towards clearer definition and more meaningful expression. It is perhaps a sign of further thought that the denial that metaphysical statements can be meaningful is no longer quite so strongly made. It is not the purpose of this paper to offer a defence of metaphysics. I merely note that metaphysical thinking is defended by Thomists as an integral part of their system of thought. St. Thomas follows Aristotle in maintaining that the first aim of philosophy is the study of being as being. His purpose is to explain existent being so far as its reality is attainable by the human mind. Differing in approach from Plato and the Neo-Platonists, he starts from the concrete, from sense perception, and by the process of abstraction strips being of its unessential notions, inquiring what being is, how it exists and what are the conditions of its existence.[1]

It is from the consideration of being as such, based on sense perception and common sense, that the Thomist rises to awareness of the supreme being, the *ipsum esse subsistens*, who is God. This is the only perfect being, the unmoved mover, the uncaused cause, the necessary and purposeful, *ens a se*. All other being is caused and contingent, eventually owing its existence to the supreme being. For the Thomist God is not only the formal cause of the universe, but the efficient cause of all that exists. Moreover he is also the final cause of creation; and all things, including man, are directed to him as their final end. This dependence on God is a fundamental point in the Thomist system. It influences Thomist teaching on all forms of human activity—moral philosophy, political philosophy and, of course, the theory of education. Man is not self-caused or self-sufficient. He is expected to live his life under the Maker's instructions.[2]

III

Once he has established the dependence of creation and of man on God, the Thomist exalts the human person as the supreme achievement in God's creation.

Man, although a dependent being, has a relative autonomy

[1] See D. J. B. Hawkins, *The Criticism of Experience*, and Maritain's fourth lecture 'Considerations about Being as Such' in *A Preface to Metaphysics*. There is an illuminating paper on 'The Function of Metaphysics' in Father Copleston's *Contemporary Philosophy*, 1956. For a fuller survey of the whole question see, for example, Mgr. L. de Raymaeker's *The Philosophy of Being*, 1954.

[2] See Hawkins, *The Essentials of Theism*, 1949; and the penetrating paper on 'The Meaning of the Terms Predicated of God' in Copleston, op. cit., pp. 87–102.

higher than that of any other creature. He is intelligent, rational, responsible and free, that is to say he is a human person. The classical definition of person has come down to us from Boethius. *Rationalis naturae individua substantia*, an individual substance of rational nature. We normally regard a person as the ultimate subject to which action and decision can be attributed, implying that the person has complete self-command and that he is the master of his own actions. Person answers the question 'Who am I?' rather than 'What am I?', and the human person being aware of his own self-identity, aware too that his actions are attributable to himself as his own, accepts responsibility for them and recognizes the rights and duties that flow from this self-possession. The person is in conscious possession of a rational nature distinct and separate from every other. 'To be oneself,' a modern Thomist has said, 'having a being of one's own, with such self-mastery as not to be under the dominion of another and not to be a part but an independent whole, this is to be a person in the full sense of the word.'[1]

St. Thomas declares that the name 'person' signifies that which is most perfect in the whole of nature and that which

[1] R. P. Phillips, *Modern Thomistic Philosophy*, Vol. II, p. 222. Cardinal Mercier put it as follows: 'An individual endowed with reason is a distinct species bearing a special name, *person*. Endowed with reason and freedom, a human individual verifies in a very special way the full self-possession that is the essence of individuality: he is unlike other individuals without reason and freedom inasmuch as he is master of his own acts and is free and independent in his direction of them towards his last end. Further, since he is responsible for his destiny he has the *right*, in the society in which he finds himself, to do and to demand whatever the achievement of his end requires; he is the subject of inviolable rights, a *moral* and *juridical* person or individual; in consequence, if reason and natural right are regarded, he may not be used as a mere tool, a thing (res), or treated, in other words, as a slave.' *A Manual of Modern Scholastic Philosophy*, Vol. I, pp. 312-13.

has the greatest nobility.[1] The perfection and nobility of the human person are rooted in his self-possession, in his dignity as a free self-directing agent. Man, in Henley's words, is master of his fate and captain of his soul. Man is, in a sense, what he makes of himself.

The activity of human persons is studied by Aquinas in the *pars secunda* of the *Summa Theologica*, and if we seek a philosophy of education in his writing it is here we must seek it.

In the first sub-division, the *prima secundae*, he deals with the pursuit of happiness, with the springs of activity, motives for human action, the appetites and internal influences which affect human conduct; the morality of human actions and habits; the rule of law in regulating human relations and the part which God plays through His grace in the human soul. In the second sub-division, the *secunda secundae*, he examines the great theological virtues of faith, hope and charity, the fundamental moral virtues of prudence, justice, fortitude and temperance, and the more perfect states of life open to human beings through the gospel message. He sets out, if you like, a blue-print for perfect human living; and its key is happiness. Happiness, St. Thomas argues, is what men strive for. It is achieved in the attainment of complete truth by the intelligence and supreme good by the will. Only in the possession of truth and good does man attain his full liberation. Nothing less gives him complete and permanent satisfaction.

---

[1] *Respondeo dicendum quod persona significat id quod est perfectissimum in tota natura, scilicet subsistens in rationali natura. S.T.* I. q. 29, art. 3.

See also *De Potentia*, q. 9, art. 3, resp.

Dicendum quod persona, sicut dictum est, significat quamdam naturam cum quodam modo existendi. Natura autem, quam persona in sua significatione includit, est omnium naturarum dignissima, scilicet natura intellectualis secundum genus suum.

The cynic might say that the Thomist system of morality is based on a sort of 'payment by results'—'Be good and you'll be happy'. This is not strictly true. It is true, however, that the system is teleological, based on final causes. The motive of human conduct is the pursuit of happiness and once the ultimate goal of happiness has been established the test of the moral quality of human actions has been laid down. Whatever is a means to that end is good; whatever is opposed to that end is evil. Properly understood the Thomist motto might well be expressed: 'Whatever makes you truly happy must be good.' But you must be sure it will make you truly and finally happy. Hence the immense importance in the Thomist system of a personal decision concerning the achievement of happiness—that stable and unshakeable possession of perfect good as St. Thomas defines it from Boethius. Here in the view of Thomas and the Thomists is the test of maturity. A man who has not yet given consideration to his final end and how it is to be obtained has not yet fully grown up. He is not fully educated. He is immature.

Because the proper object of the will is nothing less than the supreme good, the will is free in relation to lesser good. This is the psychological basis of the Thomist defence of free will, of human freedom, and at once it introduces educational principles of great importance. Because he is free, man is responsible for the attainment of his end, and one of the aims of education must be to train him in responsibility. Because the Thomist moral system is teleological, involving the attainment of an end, the understanding of interest and purpose must be included in any educational system. To some extent the why is more important than the how. St. Thomas would say that no child should be made to do a thing without understanding why he is doing it. The practice of virtue, particularly the fundamental virtues of prudence, justice, fortitude and temperance, the proper control of natural appetites by intelligence and will are necessary educational aims in such a system. Since the will seeks only the highest good, a hierarchy of values, standards of conduct, even a theory of art and craft[1] will form part of any educational system seeking Thomist approval. Thomists would endorse the statement of aims in education made by the Norwood Committee in the introduction to their Report:

We believe that education cannot stop short of recognizing the ideals of truth and beauty and goodness as final and binding for all times and in all places, as ultimate values; we do not believe that these ideals are of temporary convenience only, as devices for holding together society till they can be dispensed with as knowledge grows and organization becomes more scientific. Further, we hold that the recognition of such values implies, for most people at least, a religious interpretation of life which for us must mean the Christian interpretation of life. We have no sympathy, therefore, with a theory of education which pre-supposes that its aim can be dictated by the provisional findings of special Sciences, whether biological, psychological or sociological, that the function of education is to fit pupils to determine their outlook and conduct according to the changing

---

[1] In spite of such works as Maritain's *Art and Scholasticism* and *Art and Poetry*, or Thomas Gilby's *Poetic Experience*, it is, I think, generally admitted that in the writings of Aquinas there is no formal discussion of aesthetic theory, at least in any educational sense. Maritain notes however (and Eric Gill has supported him) that the sphere of making is the sphere of art; and that in this sphere the rules and values are those of the work to be produced rather than of the person who carries out the work. He goes on to speak of the 'despotic and all-absorbing power of art, as also its astonishing power of soothing'. The artist devotes himself 'to the service of the thing which he is making'. Here, I suggest, is the outline of a theory of art and practical activities in education and a link with at least one aspect of occupational therapy. See Maritain, *Art and Scholasticism*, p. 6. See also the article by J. Fearon 'The Lure of Beauty' in *The Thomist*, 1945, pp. 150–83; A. Nemetz, 'Art in St. Thomas Aquinas' in *The New Scholasticism*, Vol. 25, 1951, pp. 282–9.

needs and the changing standards of the day. We agree whole-heartedly that scientific method and scientific planning can do much to help in the realization of the 'good life', and education which does not avail itself of such aid denies itself one means to the realization of its ends. But our belief is that education from its own nature must be ultimately concerned with values which are independent of time or particular environment, though realizable under changing forms in both, and therefore that no programmes of education which concern themselves only with relative ends and the immediate adaptation of the individual to existing surroundings can be acceptable.[1]

The principal aim in the education of human persons should, therefore, be the conquest of freedom, inner and spiritual, by each person—or, as Maritain has put it, his 'liberation through knowledge and wisdom, good will and love'. This supposes two important elements in education. First that the horizons are wide enough for this liberty, and secondly that the teacher appreciates what the liberation of the human person really means.

IV

The whole range of knowledge, technique and art, must come within the scope of education. The Thomist will not hold with piety divorced from technique, nor technique divorced from the general influence of culture. Liberation springs from knowledge, and the first aim in education must therefore be the pursuit of knowledge and of truth. A modern Thomist has reminded us that this pursuit must take in the full range of knowledge, the secular as well as the theological. Let me refer to M. Etienne Gilson:

We have all met, either in history or indeed round about us, Christians who believe they are rendering homage to God by

[1] *Curriculum and Examinations in Secondary Schools*, H.M.S.O., p. viii.

affecting, in regard to science, philosophy, and art, an indifference which sometimes approaches contempt. But this contempt may express either supreme greatness or supreme littleness. I like to be told that all philosophy is not worth an hour of trouble, when he who tells me so is called Pascal, that is to say a man who is at once one of the greatest philosophers, one of the greatest scientists, and one of the greatest artists of all time. A person always has the right to disdain what he surpasses, especially if what he disdains is not so much the thing loved as the excessive attachment which enslaves us to it. Pascal despised neither science nor philosophy, but he never pardoned them for having once hidden from him the most profound mystery of charity. Let us be careful, therefore, we who are not Pascal, of despising what perhaps surpasses us, for science is one of the highest praises of God: the understanding of what God has made.[1]

He is tart in his comments on those who speak too glibly about the achievements of the ages of faith. 'Look around you,' they say: 'See the achievements of the ages of faith in the great cathedrals of Western Europe.' 'Sans doute,' says M. Gilson, 'but faith would have constructed nothing at all if there had not also been architects.' And if it is true that the façade of Notre Dame of Paris is a yearning of the soul toward God, that does not prevent its being also a remarkable piece of geometrical work, applied mathematics, and of the skill of the mason's craft. A great deal of hard mathematical thinking and sound building practice went into those 'dreams in stone' which are the triumph of the ages of faith.

There is a danger, on the other hand, that highly specialized scientific and technical achievement may be a hindrance to personal fulfilment. The cult of over-specialization may lead to what Maritain has called 'a progressive animalization of the human mind'; for the animal is after all a great specialist

[1] See his paper 'The Intelligence in the Service of Christ' in *A Gilson Reader*, 1957.

—as witness the ant or bee. Its energy and instincts are directed to the perfect performance of a single task. Our society may well be moving dangerously close to a situation in which we train specialists for supreme competence in a narrower and narrower field, depriving them of the possibility of passing informed judgment on anything beyond the limit of their own competence. The Thomist conception of the person revolts against the idea that a man's main pursuit in life should be narrowed and cramped in its horizons, or should be considered in terms of economic values or scientific achievement, with possibly some cheap pleasure or social entertainment to fill his leisure hours, and perhaps a vague religious feeling without intellectual content to quieten conscience. Here is danger of the dehumanized life.

The aim of education is the making of persons. The purpose of the educator should be to guide the developing nature of the child to that unique perfection which makes the self complete in its inward life. Other aims may seem of more immediate or practical importance—education for livelihood, education for leisure, education for service or for citizenship—but these must always remain secondary and subordinate to the making of persons, with their unique freedom, responsibility and immortality.

This making of persons supposes the fulfilment of the characteristic personal qualities of human nature; the fulfilment of intelligence in the attainment of truth, the satisfaction of will in the possession of perfect and stable good; the balance and poise of self-possession and a well-directed life.

It may well be argued that this high Thomist ideal is unattainable, that absolute truth and supreme good are beyond the scope of human achievement, that this is no more than a pipe dream—if you will allow the anachronism of the metaphor applied to a thirteenth-century Dominican friar. Thomists, however, accept the reality of our present condition. They recognize that these ideals are indeed difficult and perhaps impossible of attainment in the disarray and disorder of human living, where appetite and passion are so seldom subject to intelligence and will, where effort is reluctant and pride so often content with petty achievement. They would endorse the statement made in a leading article in *The Times Literary Supplement* that the fact that man so often sees and approves the better but follows the worse can be explained only by the fact of Original Sin. The ideal of personal fulfilment in truth and goodness remains constant however, and the Thomist is prepared to justify it as the true aim of education.

Whether this introduces the element of supernatural truth and of the attainment of eternal happiness must to some extent depend on religious outlook and religious faith. The Thomist who is a Catholic—and understandably so many are—will be prepared to see the fulfilment of these aims of education, perhaps only partially *per speculum in aenigmate* in man's present life, with the promise of complete and absolute fulfilment only in eternity. Maritain has not been afraid to say that the saints and martyrs are the true educators of mankind.[1]

St. Thomas follows Aristotle in arguing that every agent acts for an end and that the human agent acts for, and seeks, happiness. Happiness must consist chiefly in the activity which perfects the highest faculty in man. Hence human happiness will consist primarily in the contemplation of the highest objects. Perfect happiness can be found only in God, the perfect truth, the supreme and infinite good. Is there such a thing as natural happiness for man? Or is it true that for all men ultimate and perfect beatitude consist only in the vision of the divine essence. The answer to this question affects the whole of Thomist moral theory and passes into the

[1] *Education at the Crossroads*, p. 25.

realm of revealed religion and theology. It can have no more than a mention in the present context.[1]

[1] See L. E. O'Mahony, *The Desire of God in the Philosophy of St. Thomas.* A good summary of the question in Copleston, op. cit., Ch. xxxix. See also W. R. O'Connor, *The Eternal Quest*, 1947, and *The Natural Desire for God*, 1948.

At this stage enters the whole question of religion in education. I do not propose to discuss the question in this series dealing with philosophical aims, save to note the fundamental importance of rational convictions on this issue. The question is not one of religious sentiment or emotion, but of cold fact and argument. 'Not merely in the realm of natural theology but in the realm of revealed religion Faith is an intellectual assent to a proposition whose truth is accepted on the authority of God. The consequences, of course, are of tremendous importance, and they are bound to affect the whole of one's attitude towards education. It is either true or not true that God exists and has revealed His purpose for men through the incarnation of His Son, Jesus Christ. It is either true or not true that the human spirit is of its nature indestructible, and hence immortal; that it is superior to its worldly environment and that it reaches out to the realm of the absolute—the mind seeking absolute truth, the will seeking absolute good. The period of man's existence on earth is, as it has been put, merely a spring-board into eternity. So also it is either true or not true that there are definite maker's instructions for the running of human life—personal, domestic, social and international.

'One must reach a decision on the truth of these propositions, for on their truth or falsehood the place of religion in education necessarily depends. From these truths is drawn a philosophy of life: on them are based standards of values, religious and ethical. In function of these truths a whole philosophy of education is constructed. Nobody who holds these truths can subscribe to the near-blasphemy which pays lip-service to God for a few moments in the day and rules Him out of the remainder of human activities and calculations, or which thinks that our obligations to Him can be met merely by a collective act of worship at the beginning of a school day, and that He may be then quietly ignored in all those other subjects which contribute to the flowering of culture and the development of character. We refuse to think of God as some of the disciples of Newton are reputed to have thought of Him—as a being whose intervention in the cosmic order provided a handy explanation for discrepancies in the Newtonian system—a dignified cosmic

V

The aim of education must include some reference to the importance of the teacher, and the function of the teacher in education has its place in Thomist philosophy. Two characteristics of that philosophy are its teaching on matter and form and on the passage from potency to act. Every process, every development in nature is a passage from potentiality to activity, from possibility to actuality. Equally everything which exists does so in virtue of the two-fold principle of matter and form, form being the determining principle which makes an individual what it is, while matter establishes it as an individual.

St. Thomas also accepted from Aristotle the four-fold division of causes: the material cause—the out-of-what a thing is made; the formal cause—the into-what a thing is made; the efficient cause or the how of its making; and the final cause or the why of its making.

Although St. Thomas wrote no formal treatise on education, he applies these principles not only to his theory of knowledge but to the educational process. For the Thomist the aim of education is to draw out human potentiality to perfection and activity in the full human person. So the

---

plumber, it has been said, going about mending leaks in the Newtonian Universe.

'The purpose of education is to fit men and women for life, and the purpose of this life, so we hold, is to fit them for eternity. The first function of Christian education, then, is to impart a knowledge of God and of God's revelation—of Christ as the way, the truth, and the life, of the truth to be lived and the means of living it. Man is made by God and for God and his ultimate destiny is either supreme happiness or complete frustration. If I may put it this way, life must always be a fascinating game because it is a game being played for eternal stakes.' See *Religion in Education* by the present writer, pp. 8–9.

child is the material cause, the pupil's self-activity is the efficient cause, the integrated and liberated human person is the formal cause, while the ideal which the educational system presents is the final cause of the educational achievement—as the Catholic Thomist would express it, the vision of God.

In his treatise *De Magistro* St. Thomas begins by asking if one man can teach another and he immediately proposes certain difficulties. Man can teach men he points out only by signs or symbols—speech, writing, language, visual aids —and the mere proposing of symbols does not convey knowledge. If I propose a symbol, the pupil either knows what it signifies or he does not. If he knows already, I teach him nothing. If he does not know, the significance of the symbol escapes him. Teachers of language particularly of the nuances in foreign language and literature will appreciate the difficulty which St. Thomas exposes.

It is in fact the intellect which knows and since teaching can be carried out only by means of sensible symbols teaching cannot of itself effectively produce new intellectual knowledge in the pupil's mind. The statement may seem paradoxical, but what takes place in education is not that the teacher teaches, but that the pupil learns. Education is possible only because the human person possesses an active potentiality for knowledge. It is by reason of an inner vital dynamism of mind that union between the intellect and its object is achieved. The living principle of knowledge is within the pupil. He is the active agent in the process of education. The teacher's function is above all to stimulate this activity:

St. Thomas would have had no sympathy with any system of forcing or cramming or conditioning; with any system which would relegate the learner to a subordinate place in the teacher-pupil relationship or reduce education to mere instruction.

Furthermore, the fact that the mind's potency is active means that, according to Thomistic principles, and absolutely speaking, it can, independently, promote itself to complete actualization. Nevertheless, this potency is real and not simply a figure of speech: the mind is in essential, not merely in accidental, potency before the knowledge to be acquired. St. Thomas clarifies this distinction by his comparison of reason with the sense of sight. The visual sense, and indeed all the senses, are in accidental potency before their objects. The eye knows intuitively the objects which it sees; a simple direction towards the visible thing is sufficient for the identification of sense knowledge. Reason cannot travel by this royal road: reason is a *vis collativa*, a discursive power, moving forward by inference and deduction. The reason's ignorance, therefore, is an essential potency: to this there must correspond an essential mover.[1]

This does not mean that the teacher has no part to play in the educational process. St. Thomas likens the work of the teacher to that of the doctor in the healing of a patient. The sick man is not merely a passive recipient of medical attention. He is in active potentiality with regard to health. His own inner principle of health is the primary cause of his cure: the doctor's part being to assist nature to cure itself. In a similar way the teacher administers to the learner's mind. He contributes judgment, intellectual skill and understanding, but his role is a secondary or a ministerial one. The pupil's intelligence is the primary cause of his intellectual advancement.

Yet the comparison between the doctor and the teacher is an inadequate one, and the teacher's assistance in the educational process is deeper and more personal than the part played by the doctor in promoting a cure. A doctor who is

[1] Rev. G. J. Shannon, 'Aquinas on the Teacher's Art' in the *Clergy Review*, June 1949. See also Rev. T. Corbishley, S.J., 'St. Thomas and Educational Theory' in the *Dublin Review*, January 1943.

himself sick can promote a cure if his medical knowledge is sufficient. The teacher on the other hand requires full possession of the entire knowledge, possession of which he wishes to stimulate in the pupil. Skill in method is not enough. The teacher's mind must embrace the whole field of the subject he professes to teach. It has been well said that a diseased doctor can cure the sick if he knows his medicine; an ignorant teacher however well trained cannot teach.

Hence for the Thomist not only possession of the subject he professes, but the right co-ordination of knowledge and a proper scale of values are essential for the teacher. This is one of the reasons why Catholic parents insist that their children should be entrusted in school to Catholic teachers. The teacher's causality in the educational process has results in terms of appreciation of truth, natural and supernatural, standards of values, moral, aesthetic and literary which depend ultimately on the personality of the teacher himself. The Norwood Committee suggested that a broad education 'might be based upon very few subjects handled by a teacher with breadth of outlook', and went on to say that the integration of the curriculum was not a means, let alone an end, in education:

If anything is to be integrated, it is not the curriculum that must be integrated, but the personality of the child: and this can be brought about, not by adjustment of subjects as such, but by the realization of his purpose as a human being, which in turn can be brought about only by contact with minds conscious of a purpose for him. Only the teacher can make a unity of a child's education by promoting the unity of his personality in terms of purpose.[1]

That unity of the child's personality will be a reflection of the unity, balance and poise of the personality of the teacher, and this will depend on a whole philosophy and outlook on life.

[1] *Curriculum and Examinations in Secondary Schools*, H.M.S.O., p. 61.

The point is made very clearly in the Ministry of Education's pamphlet No. 31 on *Health Education*:

Teachers, therefore, occupy a place of prime importance in the nurturing and furtherance of good mental health in children. In the first place, the teacher's own personality is of the greatest possible importance. Unless he has himself reached an emotional maturity which is stable and healthy, he is not equipped to exert the right influence on the receptive child. For he possesses such a vital power in the shaping of the child's personality that what he is himself cannot help making a very significant impression for good or ill upon most of the children in his care. Therefore, he should know himself.[1]

He must have that maturity about which I spoke earlier in this paper. He should have decided about his last end. He should know where he is going.

A wise and famous Head Master once said that the rules for a schoolmaster were as simple to state as they were hard to fulfil: they were only that he should know what he wanted his boys to know, that he should be what he wanted his boys to be, and that he should add enthusiasm.[2]

VI

In the social order, man's role is more complex, and it is in the field of sociology and political philosophy that modern Thomists have made some of their most important contributions to educational thought.[3]

[1] *Health Education*, H.M.S.O., pp. 157–8.
[2] Norwood Report, p. 87.
[3] See Maritain, *Freedom in the Modern World*, 1935; *Scholasticism and Politics*, 1940; *The Person and the Common Good*, 1941; *The Rights of Man and Natural Law*, 1943; *Man and the State*, 1954: Thomas Gilby, *Between Community and Society*, 1953; *Principality and Polity*, 1958: M. de Wulf, *Philosophy and Civilization in the Middle Ages*, 1922.

On the one hand, man is part of a social community and, as such, is inferior to it and bound to serve its ends, even, if necessary, to the sacrifice of his life. On the other hand, he is a person with an immortal soul and, as such, of more importance than anything else in the world.[1]

How must a man consider himself with regard to society and his fellows? Is he merely part of a whole to serve the interests of the whole? Must he accept the utilitarian principle of the greatest good of the greatest number? Or will he proclaim the Rousseauist doctrine that all things are permissible to him which do not harm another? The Thomist sees the key to these complex social relations in the attainment of what St. Thomas calls the common good, which is at once personal and social.

Maritain says:

If man is naturally a political animal, this is so in the sense that society, required by nature, is achieved through free consent, and because the human person demands the communications of social life through the openness and generosity proper to intelligence and love as well as through the needs of a human individual born

[1] ' "L'homme est tout entier partie de la communauté politique, mais il n'est pas partie de la communauté politique selon lui-même tout entier et selon tout ce qui est en lui; il y a en lui des biens qui dépassent cette communauté et auxquels la communauté elle-même doit servir; son âme immortelle et son Dieu ne sont pas au service de l'Etat." ' Maritain *Sort de l'Homme*, p. 61, quoted by N. W. Michener, *Maritain on the Nature of Man*, p. 93.

Two typical texts of St. Thomas are worth quoting: 'Quaelibet autem persona singularis comparatur ad totam communitatem sicut pars ad totum.' IIa, IIae, 64. 2.

'Homo non ordinatur ad communitatem politicam secundum se totum et secundum omnia sua . . . sed totum, quod homo est et quod habet ordinandum est ad Deum.' Ia, IIae, 21. 4. ad 3.

See the remarkable Glossary published by Father Eschmann in *Medieval Studies* (Toronto), Vol. V, 1943.

naked and destitute. Thus it is that social life tends to emancipate man from the bondage of material nature. It subordinates the individual to the common good, but always in order that the common good flow back upon the individuals, and that they enjoy that freedom of expansion or independence which is insured by the economic guarantees of labour and ownership, political rights, civil virtues, and the cultivation of the mind.[1]

The ultimate end of education, in the Thomist view, concerns the human person in his personal life and not in relation to his social environment, yet the perfection of the person has its reflection in the perfection of society, for human society is a group of human freedoms in action with and respecting each other. What matters about the good citizen is not the externals of his behaviour but the inner core of his conscience. A society of conformists is not necessarily a healthy society, as we know only too well from the totalitarian experiences of modern times. What matters is 'the living source of personal conscience in which originate idealism and generosity, the sense of law and the sense of friendship, respect for others but at the same time deeprooted independence with regard to common opinion'.[2]

I would refer you on this point to the Riddell Memorial Lecture given by the Principal of the University of Aberdeen in Durham in 1954 under the title *The Discipline of Virtue*. Sir Thomas Murray Taylor speaks as follows:

It is a constant theme with the masters of political wisdom from Milton to Acton that political liberty is something which depends ultimately on the moral qualities of the citizens. How is it possible, asked de Tocqueville, that society should escape destruction, if the moral tie be not strengthened, in proportion

---

[1] *Education at the Crossroads*, p. 14. See also S. Michel, *La Notion Thomiste du Bien Commun*.

[2] Maritain, ibid., p. 16.

as the political tie is relaxed? In *The Excursion* Wordsworth put it thus:

> The discipline of slavery is unknown
> Among us—hence the more do we require
> The discipline of virtue; order else
> Cannot subsist nor confidence nor peace.

It was the same truth which Burke expressed in the *Letter to a Member of the National Assembly*:

Men are qualified for civil liberty in exact proportion to their disposition to put moral chains upon their own appetites; in proportion as their love of justice is above their rapacity; in proportion as their soundness and sobriety of understanding is above their vanity and presumption; in proportion as they are more disposed to listen to the counsel of the wise and good in preference to the flattery of knaves. Society cannot exist unless a controlling power upon will and appetite be placed somewhere, and the less of it there is within, the more there must be without. It is ordained in the eternal constitution of things that men of intemperate minds cannot be free. Their passions forge their fetters.[1]

What Burke said is really the summary of the Thomist aim in education. It supposes the development of human personality in sobriety of understanding, in wisdom, the love of justice and self-discipline. From that personal development, whose core is conscience, come the origins of the good society and healthy social life. A good society will be a society of fully developed persons. Though difficult indeed of attainment, that remains the Thomist aim.

[1] Sir Thomas Murray Taylor, *The Discipline of Virtue*, p. 9.

INDEX

INDEX

INDEX